George Braziller, Inc., New York 1962

The visual craft of William Golden

Editors: Cipe Pineles Golden, Kurt Weihs, Robert Strunsky

The editors wish to acknowledge their deep obligation to the many friends and associates of William Golden whose generous assistance has made the preparation of this volume a truly cooperative enterprise. Particular thanks is due Fred W. Friendly who first proposed and set in motion the procedures for its publication.

Special acknowledgement equally must be given to Edward W. Side, Production Manager of the Advertising and Sales Promotion Department of the CBS Television Network, without whose untiring efforts and devotion the successful completion of this book would not have been achieved. Indeed, much of the quality of the original material contained herein can be attributed to his exceptional production skills, knowledge and experience as a longtime colleague of William Golden.

The editors would also like to express their gratitude to Joseph Blumenthal, Ruth Cannon, Tom Courtos, Estelle Ellis, Joe Kaufman, Teri Kerner, Mort Rubenstein, Ezra Stoller, Constance Styler and Helen Valentine—as well as to Columbia Broadcasting System, Inc. for permission to reproduce the pictorial material in this book.

For information address the publisher
George Braziller, Inc.
215 Park Avenue South, New York 3

First Printing
Library of Congress Catalog
Card No. 62-9694
Printed in the United States of America

For Tom Golden

William Golden was born and brought up in the Lower East Side of Manhattan as the youngest in a family of twelve children. His formal schooling ended after he attended the Vocational School for Boys, where he was taught photo-engraving and the rudiments of commercial design.

He spent the first few years of his professional life in Los Angeles working in lithography and photo-engraving plants. From there, he moved to the art department of the *Los Angeles Examiner* where he designed newspaper advertisements. A few years later he returned to New York where he became a member of the promotion department of the *Journal-American*.

The turning point of his career came when his talents were spotted by Dr. M. F. Agha, the noted Art Director of Condé Nast publications, who invited him to join *House and Garden*. After serving an apprenticeship under Dr. Agha who, in Golden's own words "... forced the people who worked for him to try constantly to surpass themselves," he left in 1937 to join the Columbia Broadcasting System. Three years later he was appointed Art Director of CBS.

On October 11, 1942 he married Cipe Pineles; their son, Thomas, was born on March 30, 1951. In 1942 Golden took a leave of absence from CBS to work in the Office of War Information in Washington, D.C., and a year later entered the United States Army as a private. After serving as Art Director of Army training manuals in Washington and, later in Europe, with the Army's Education and Information Division, he was discharged in 1946 with the rank of Captain. He resumed work at CBS, and in 1951 became Creative Director of Advertising and Sales Promotion for the CBS Television Network.

William Golden's work has been exhibited extensively in Europe as well as throughout the United States. He was twice chosen as one of the "ten best" art directors by the National Society of Art Directors and over the years received the prime awards of various graphic exhibitions throughout the nation. He was a member of the Board of Directors of the American Institute of Graphic Arts and, as Chairman of its "Design and Printing for Commerce" exhibition, inaugurated the celebrated "Fifty Advertisements of the Year" show.

In 1958 a collection of his work was exhibited at the White Museum of Art at Cornell University. In 1959, shortly after his death, he was chosen as "Art Director of the Year" by the National Society of Art Directors.

Contents

List of Illustrations

Preface

by Frank Stanton

For nearly a quarter of a century, William Golden was associated with CBS. I worked with him. I knew him. He was my friend. During all that time, he had one devotion and that was to excellence.

Bill Golden's passion for excellence was quiet and deep. It ran through everything he touched. It governed his daily work, his relationships to others, his career, his life. It was his life. He could not have cared less about titles or rank or position. He respected quality wherever he found it, and in design he was absolutely uncompromising as far as quality was concerned. There was no factor, no person, no compulsion that would lead him to settle for the second best.

Those who tried (and most tried only once) by argument or by stratagem to get him to go along with less than what he thought was possible, or to discard what he knew was good, never got away with it. Bill could be inflexible, abrupt, impatient. But he was also gentle, kind and warm. He could not be bargained with or cowed. There was fibre in his character—a tough fibre that won him the respect of all his colleagues.

CBS has a very deep and a very real obligation to Bill Golden
—and so, by extension, does all advertising. Bill believed that the way to command attention and win approval was not by being sensational or shrill or obvious, but by being distinguished and subtle and original. This book, indeed, is an anthology of how to achieve distinction through unfailing good taste.

Distinction in advertising was a quality essential to the growth of CBS. As media ourselves, we could not afford to place in other advertising media less than first-rate art and copy. Bill Golden was our relentless master in the pursuit of the first-rate. He knew that it did not come as easily as the adequate. He himself labored long hours to achieve the best—a perfectionist as demanding of himself as he was of others.

Bill's life was short. Bill's life was full. His was a powerful influence that went out way beyond those of us who were prodded into doing our best by the very proximity of his vigorous personality. His influence reached out to creative forces in graphics everywhere, bringing them into new fields and, even more important, giving them new standards of excellence.

I hope very much that Bill Golden's influence will be extended and prolonged by these examples of his brilliant work.

The passionate eye

by Will Burtin

Consider this:
...a period in history marked by deep conflicts between ideas, social theories, people and interests ... a period marked by a technological progress held inconceivable only two decades ago ...a period of falling idols and new heroes...an epoch when a new communication medium takes a powerful hold on people's consciousness of the world around them ...

...a corporation that grows within a lifetime from small beginnings to giant size — with correspondents, camera crews, commentators around the globe to respond on the spot to significant events wherever they happen ... a corporation whose business is: the presentation of entertainment, the news and its interpretation, and the sale of air time to advertisers ...a corporation that sends sound and images into homes, plants, offices, restaurants, theatres—indeed, wherever there are people to receive them...

...a professional field of extreme competitiveness, filled with people of strong words and often changing convictions ...a field crisscrossed by the plowed furrows of surveys, visual formulas, slogans and the hard-sell techniques of a commercial age ...a field in which every aspect of art, human aspirations and emotions, historic events, science, has been used to produce some of the most inspiring and memorable experiences, as well as rivers of mediocrity and worse...

...a man who never forgets: that he is responsible for what he does and what his work may do for others; that a moral question stands behind every moment of living and working; that the corporation which employs his skill is a combination of people with many abilities and motivations but one purpose; that giving a unifying visual face to this purpose is his job as art director.

His eye is unerring. His designs hit the bull's eye of a target with that deceptive ease which only the strong can command. They are based on an instinct that would make a journalist envious. He has a sense for the explosive impact of words. He understands the relationship between an artist's personality, his style, his potential and how these factors will result in an original expression that gives new meaning to a message. There is a mental dexterity and an absolute mastery of subtle details, a complete absence of graphic tricks or of intellectual gimmickry, which brings admiration wherever his work ap-

pears. But above all there is a passion for everything that has to do with his job — for the corporation he works for, for the message he develops and designs, for the people who work with him and the people he addresses his work to, for the means he employs—be they the paper a design is printed on or the type face and size used, the halftone screen or the subject and style of art work—nothing escapes this intensive attention. The success of this working method has made advertising and design history. There are many medals, awards, magazine articles, letters, speeches, reprints of work. Unmoved by laudatory exclamations every new job reflects his deeper insight into the fabric of human communication and motivation.

Little is known about the demanding realities behind this prestige: the unending pressure of daily deadlines, of big ads, of small ads, big folders, small folders, of books and pamphlets, of annual reports, styling of studio fronts, the development of "the eye" as a CBS trademark—the conscious application of the trademark in steadily changing ways—the unending concern with new ways to say something still simpler, stronger, more beautiful!

In our design schools we teach the meaning of esthetics, we define rules of design, we teach working procedures. But what we cannot teach is the feeling for continuity, how to remain alert to the sudden excitement of a better idea two hours before the engraver picks up the completed art work, how to keep a staff electrified and unified in the dedication to perfection, how to solve the problems of a "corporate image" by conceiving of it as the grand design behind individual designs and not as a mere variation of a principle—and how to, at the same time, watch news reports, sales reports, program developments, listen to meanings behind the words of the great and the small.

He is used to tough work, tough words and tough conditions. What he knows is self-taught. His scorn for the self-centered, socially ambitious and security-craving is genuine. He wants achievement, not publicity. He wants to see work and not a tricky paste-up of other people's work. He distrusts a formula and respects only unreserved attention to a task, in which no detail is small or without significance.

His is the kind of full dedication that tells all who know him and his work that here is a real teacher, a real professional, a friend and a man. Here is William Golden.

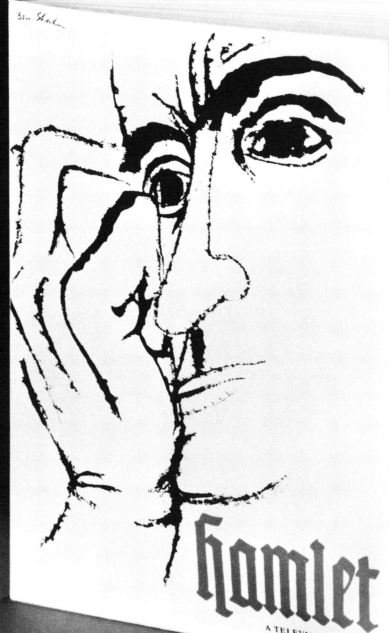

(On April 18, 1959 The Type Directors Club of New York invited thirteen leading art directors and designers, including William Golden, to participate in a forum entitled "Typography—U.S.A." at the Hotel Biltmore. A booklet was subsequently issued containing the views of each member of the panel, including the following statement by Mr. Golden.)

Type is to read

If there is such a thing as a "New American Typography" surely it speaks with a foreign accent. And it probably talks too much. Much of what it says is obvious nonsense. A good deal of it is so pompous that it sounds like nonsense, though if you listen very carefully it isn't . . . quite. It is just overcomplicated. When it is translated into prewar English it is merely obvious.

I don't know what it is that impels so many designers to drop their work to write and speak so much about design.

Is it the simple (and perfectly justifiable) instinct for trade promotion? Or have we imported the European propensity for surrounding even the simplest actions with a *gestalt?*

Perhaps the explanation is simpler. The kind of effort that goes into graphic expression is essentially lonely and intensive, and produces, at its best, a simple logical design. It is sometimes frustrating to find that hardly anyone knows that it is a very complicated job to produce something simple. Per-

The design of this 112-page book, illustrated with drawings by Ben Shahn, was based on a 78-minute script, adapted from the three-hour original play of The Old Vic Company

13

Takes the skull.

Alas, poor Yorick!
I knew him, Horatio—a fellow of infinite jest, of most excellent fancy.

He hath bore me on his back a thousand times, and now how abhorred in my imagination it is!

My gorge rises at it. Here hung those lips that I have kiss'd I know not how oft!

Where be your gibes now? Your gambols, your songs, your flashes of merriment, that were wont to set the table on a roar? Not one now to mock your own grinning, quite chop-fallen.

haps we want them to know that we've gone through hell, sweating out a job to reach what seems to be an obvious solution.

And since our professional medium of communication is not verbal, designers don't seem to be lucid writers or speakers on the subject of design.

I have been frequently stimulated by the work of most of the people on this panel, but only rarely by what they have said about it.

While it must be assumed that these endless discussions have values that I am blind to, I am more acutely aware of the dangers they hold for the young. If you have recently interviewed a crop of young designers—the New Renaissance Man in a hurry—applying for their first or second staff job, you will know what I mean.

I was forced to part with one such man on my staff a while ago. He was pretty good, too. But he was another victim of the overseriousness of graphic arts literature. He had all the latest and obscure publications from here and abroad (mostly in languages he couldn't read). He attended all the forums. He would argue endlessly on theory . . . and he was just paralyzed with fright at the sight of a blank layout pad. He could spend as much as a week on a 50-line newspaper ad. His trouble was, that no matter how he tried, an ad looked very much like an ad, and not any of these almost mystical things he had been reading about.

If there were some way to fix an age limit for attendance at these conferences, in the way that minors are forbidden to attend overstimulating movies, I think they would be relatively harmless, and it might even be pleasant to chew our cud together.

For it has all been said, and said many times, and in a most

The typographic styling—
Times Roman for text,
italics in red for stage directions—
the pacing and scale of the 35 drawings,
give new emphasis to a timeless drama

PLAYHOUSE 90 PRESENTS **ERNEST HEMINGWAY'S** CLASSIC OF ADVENTURE, LOVE AND DEATH IN THE SPANISH CIVIL WAR FOR WHOM THE BELL TOLLS **STARRING MARIA SCHELL, JASON ROBARDS, JR., MAUREEN STAPLETON** AND SPECIAL GUEST STAR ELI WALLACH, 9:30 TO II PM CNYT PART I: MARCH I2, PART 2: MARCH I9, I959 CBS◉

8 to 9 tonight CBS ◉ channel 2—an exciting event on the

ED SULLIVAN SHOW
Don't miss the unprecedented full-hour rebroadcast of the world famous
MOISEYEV DANCERS
"the most electrifying exhibition of folk dancing ever seen on television"

*Whether a promotion kit cover
shows a Shahn portrait of Hemingway,
or a newspaper ad a stock photo,
the design objective is the same:*

*To create immediate understanding
of a significant event,
even before one line has been read*

U. N. Conference Room

A TELEVISION NOTEBOOK

with drawings by Henry Koerner

CBS TELEVISION NETWORK

1959

THE GENEVA CONFERENCE

On the eve of the historic East-West Foreign Ministers' meeting, CBS NEWS gathers six top correspondents in Geneva: HOWARD K. SMITH and ERIC SEVAREID from Washington, CHARLES COLLINGWOOD from London, DAVID SCHOENBRUN from Paris, ERNEST LEISER from Bonn and DANIEL SCHORR on assignment to Warsaw, for a special on-the-scene report that examines the Berlin crisis, the bargaining positions of East and West and the possible outcome of the discussions in the Palais des Nations.

5-6 PM WCBS-TV ⓢ channel 2

The international scene is a frequent subject for advertisements.

A familiar typographic "SEE" column is given added impact by its frame of massed photography.

The photograph of Khrushchev, taken from the television screen, reflects the urgency of the message

confusing way, and almost none of it is new. Even the insistence on newness at any cost is in itself familiar.

Perhaps it would be useful for a conference like this to sort it all out. Not merely to summarize this conference, but all of them. If it could be done without padding, I imagine that what is valid about typography would be very brief and relatively simple.

What is right about current typography is so apparent when you see it that it requires no explanation. What is wrong is a little more complex.

It is not as difficult to define what is wrong as it is to find how we got there.

I have my own notion of how we got where we are, and though I have neither the competence nor the ambition to be a typographic historian, this is roughly how it looks from one viewpoint.

Some thirty years ago the rebellious advertising and editorial designer in America was engaged in a conspiracy to bring order, clarity and directness to the printed page. He fought against the picture of the factory, the company logotype, and the small picture of the package that invariably accompanied it. He protested that the copy was too long, and that he was obliged to set it so small that no one would read it. He argued that the normal ad contained too many elements. (He even invented the "busy" page in some effort to accommodate himself to it.) He insisted that this effort to say so many things at once was self-defeating and could only result in communicating nothing to the reader.

He was essentially picture-minded, and only reluctantly realized that he had to learn something about type. It was and still is a damned nuisance, but when he realized how thoroughly its mechanical and thoughtless application could de-

WOMAN by Joe Kaufman

*A mailing piece combines
famous comments on women
by eight historic literary figures
with reviews of
a new documentary program
called "Woman!"
Full color painting
by Joe Kaufman*

stroy communication of an idea, he had to learn to control it—to design with it.

More and more typography was designed on a layout pad rather than in metal. Perhaps the greatest change in American typography was caused by this simple act—the transfer of the design function of the printer to the graphic designer.

The designer was able to bring a whole new background and a new set of influences to the printed page. He could "draw" a page. There was more flexibility in the use of a pencil than in the manipulation of a metal form. It became a new medium for the designer.

Under the twin impact of the functionalism of the Bauhaus and the practical demands of American business, the designer was beginning to learn to use the combination of word and image to communicate more effectively.

Under the influence of the modern painters, he became aware (perhaps too aware) of the textural qualities and color values of type as an element of design.

And surely a dominating influence on American typography in the prewar years was exerted by the journalists.

Newspapers and magazines were the primary media of mass communication. The skillful development of the use of headline and picture was a far more prevalent influence than the European poster. The newspaper taught us speed in communication. Everyone knew instinctively what the journalists had reduced to a formula: that if you read a headline, a picture, and the first three paragraphs of any story you would know all the essential facts.

The magazine communicated at a more leisurely pace and could be more provocative since it addressed a more selective audience. Because the magazine dealt more in concepts than in news it was far more imaginative. There was more oppor-

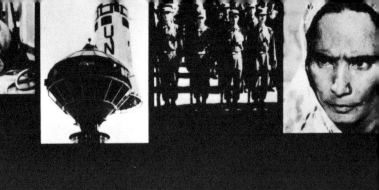

CBS Report

*Cover of a brochure
announcing a series
of documentary programs*

*Announcement folder
for the first program of "Woman!"
with a Botticelli engraving
of Venus*

tunity here, to design within the framework of the two-page spread. But still, the device that bore the main burden of interesting the reader, was the "terrific headline" and the "wonderful picture."

Perhaps it was the growth of radio, a rival medium, that hastened a new effort on the part of the magazine.

Certainly the new technical developments in photography increased the range of its reportage.

But what gave it a new direction and style was not so purely American. I think it was men like Agha and Brodovitch. These importations from Europe set a pace that not only changed the face of the magazine and consequently advertising design, but they changed the status of the designer. They did this by the simple process of demonstrating that the designer could also think.

The "layout man" was becoming an editor. He was no longer that clever, talented fellow in the back room who made a writer's copy more attractive by arranging words and pictures on the printed page in some ingenious way. He could now read and understand the text. He could even have an opinion about it. He might even be able to demonstrate that he could communicate its content better and with more interest than the writer. He could even startle the editor by suggesting content. It wasn't long before he began to design the page before it was written, and writers began to write to a character count to fit the layout.

Whatever successes this revolution achieved were accomplished by demonstration—by individual designers proving to their clients and employers (by solving their problems) the validity of their point of view and the value of their talents. It was accomplished without a single design conference in New York or in Colorado or anywhere else in America.

36
24
36
62,000,000

These are the pertinent dimensions of the young lady from Natchez when she became the new Miss America on the night of September 12.

Because it happens at a time when a new television season is just beginning, this annual contest has come to be a measure of television itself.

The 62 million viewers who witnessed the coronation of Miss America (and the introduction of the new products of the Philco Corporation) constituted the largest audience in the history of the ceremonies.

At the time of the broadcast three out of every four television homes in the country had their sets turned on —*and two out of the three were watching Miss America.*

In the past year the number of television homes increased again—by 2%. *And the audience to this CBS Television Network broadcast was greater by 7%.*

These measurements of the first special broadcast of the new season reflect not only television's constantly increasing dimensions, but the ability of the CBS Television Network to continue to attract the largest audiences in television.

It is the first clear sign that the nation's viewers and advertisers will be getting more out of television this year than ever before.

CBS

*A double-spread
trade paper advertisement
dramatizes the size
of the program's audience
through its headline.*

*A narrow newspaper ad
invites attention
to seasonal entertainment
with casual effectiveness*

There were, of course, exhibitions and award luncheons. But the exhibitions were an extension of the process of demonstration, and the arrangers of the award luncheons by some lucky instinct seldom permitted the designer to speak about his work, but rather forced the businessman to discuss it.

But more than any other single factor, I believe the designer won his new status in the business community because he had demonstrated that he could communicate an idea or a fact on the printed page at least as well, and often better, than the writer, the client, or his representative. And he could demonstrate this only if he was at least as faithful to content as he was to style.

During the war and for some time afterward, American typographers made great strides in relation to the Europeans, for the simple reason, I suppose, that there was not only a shortage of paper in Europe but there was a shortage of design. The printers and designers were in foxholes, concentration camps, or dead, and presses and foundries were being bombed.

There was a long period when the bulk of the world's graphic material was being produced in America. Though there was something approaching a paper shortage here, too, there was an excess of profits available to spend on advertising. There were few products to advertise and therefore very little to say about them. But since it was relatively inexpensive to keep a company name in print, it didn't matter too greatly what or how it was said. We produced such a volume of printed material for so long a time, that we were able to assimilate a vast amount of prewar European design, and adapt it to our own language and uses. It had become such a familiar idiom with us that it is now hardly surprising that the announcement of

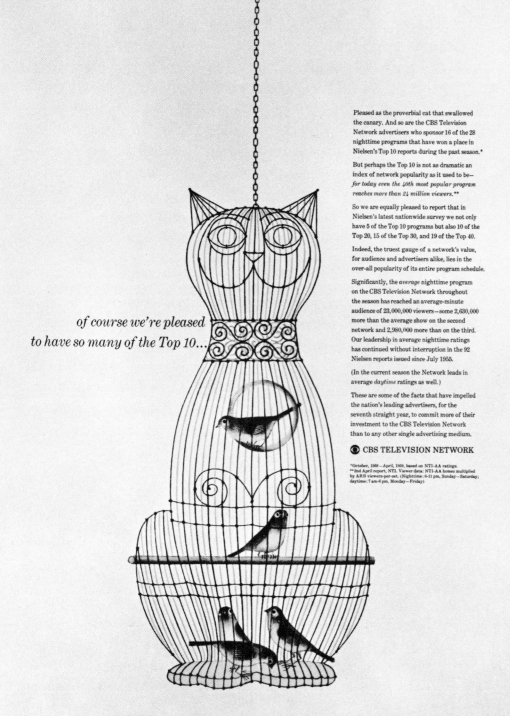

*of course we're pleased
to have so many of the Top 10...*

Pleased as the proverbial cat that swallowed
the canary. And so are the CBS Television
Network advertisers who sponsor 16 of the 28
nighttime programs that have won a place in
Nielsen's Top 10 reports during the past season.*

But perhaps the Top 10 is not as dramatic an
index of network popularity as it used to be—
*for today even the 40th most popular program
reaches more than 24 million viewers.***

So we are equally pleased to report that in
Nielsen's latest nationwide survey we not only
have 5 of the Top 10 programs but also 10 of the
Top 20, 15 of the Top 30, and 19 of the Top 40.

Indeed, the truest gauge of a network's value,
for audience and advertisers alike, lies in the
over-all popularity of its entire program schedule.

Significantly, the *average* nighttime program
on the CBS Television Network throughout
the season has reached an average-minute
audience of 23,000,000 viewers—some 2,630,000
more than the average show on the second
network and 2,980,000 more than on the third.
Our leadership in average nighttime ratings
has continued without interruption in the 92
Nielsen reports issued since July 1955.

(In the current season the Network leads in
average *daytime* ratings as well.)

These are some of the facts that have impelled
the nation's leading advertisers, for the
seventh straight year, to commit more of their
investment to the CBS Television Network
than to any other single advertising medium.

Ⓒ **CBS TELEVISION NETWORK**

*October, 1958—April, 1959, based on NTI-AA ratings.
**(2nd April report, NTI. Viewer data: NTI-AA homes multiplied
by ARB viewers-per-set. (Nighttime: 6-11 pm, Sunday—Saturday;
daytime: 7 am-6 pm, Monday—Friday)

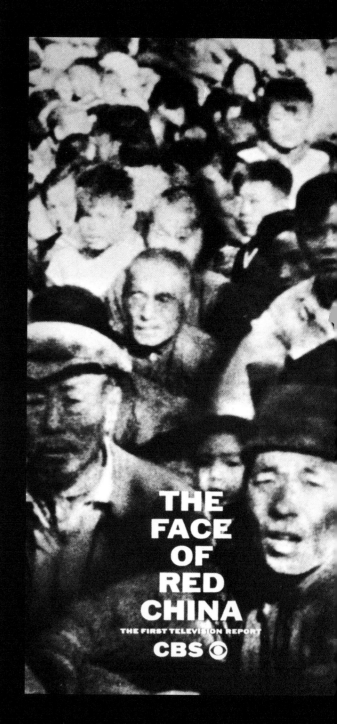

THE
FACE
OF
RED
CHINA
THE FIRST TELEVISION REPORT
CBS Ⓒ

CHARLES COLLINGWOOD brings you an exciting report from the frontiers of science—great new experiments that disclose the true qualities of MOTHER LOVE **CONQUEST** SEE THE SEASON'S PREMIERE 5:00 PM TODAY CBS ⊙ CHANNEL 2

The network's leadership
is emphasized by a whimsical drawing
in a trade advertisement...

The cover of a book
containing the full script carries out
the starkness of the documentary program...

A newspaper ad accents
a new science series with an unusual image
from the first program

this conference can call contemporary typography purely American.

My first look at postwar typography was fairly bewildering. I had seen and applauded the prewar work by Burtin and Beall. They were developing newer graphic forms, and using words and images on the printed page to communicate. In their hands these images were employed to make a statement clearer, faster.

The new avant-garde was saying nothing and saying it with considerable facility. They could say in their defense that the world was more chaotic than ever, that nobody was saying anything very rational, and that their need to make some kind of order was satisfied to some extent, by creating it on the printed page. It was, largely, an order without content.

There was precedent for this point of view. The determined sales promotion campaign of the abstract expressionist painters was in full swing in America. That it could have been so successful so quickly must surely be due, in part, to its absence of content. In a curious way this revolution was a remarkably safe one—it was so noncommittal.

I have no quarrel with the abstract movement—except with its vociferous intolerance of any other school. But I think the effect on the minds of young designers is a matter of concern. To regard the blank rectangle on a layout pad with the same attitude that the abstract painter confronts his blank canvas is surely a pointless delusion.

The printed page is not primarily a medium for self-expression. Design for print is not Art. At best it is a highly skilled craft. A sensitive, inventive, interpretive craft, if you will, but in no way related to painting.

A graphic designer is employed, for a certain sum of money, by someone who wants to say something in print to

For insertion Sunday, March 30, 1958
5 cols. x 125 lines = 625 lines
Position Request: Television Listings page.

SEE IT NOW with Edward R. Murrow reports on the question troubling people all over the world—

FALLOUT

In Part II of "Atomic Timetable" a group of world famous scientists present their conclusions on the effects of atomic radiation caused by nuclear explosions today and for future generations. Don't fail to tune to the CBS Television Network today from 5 to 6:25 ⓒ **CHANNEL 2**

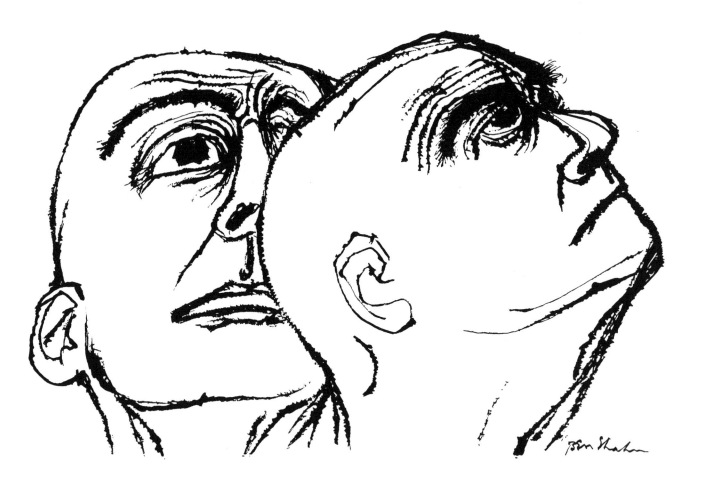

Design and art work
of two program advertisements
underscore human concern
and technical achievement

somebody. The man with something to say comes to the designer in the belief that the designer with his special skills will say it more effectively for him.

It sometimes develops that as a result of this hopeful transaction, the statement becomes an advertisement for the designer rather than his client. And should there be any doubt about the designer's intention, he will sign it—just as the easel painter does.

Logically enough, this attitude toward design is only tolerated when the client has nothing to say. When his product is no different than anyone else's, and no better. When his company has no "personality"—he borrows the personality of the designer. This is rarely permitted in the mainstream of advertising, but only in the "off-Broadway" arenas.

The immature avant-garde designer seems bitter about the mainstream of American advertising. He hates the "hard sell" and avoids clients who interfere with his freedom. He believes that the role of business should be one of patron of the Arts, and insists that his craft is art.

I do not argue for the return to any form of traditionalism. I do argue for a sense of responsibility on the part of the designer, and a rational understanding of his function.

I think he should avoid designing for designers.

I suggest that the word "design" be considered as a verb in the sense that we design something to be communicated to someone.

Perhaps it would help to clear the air a little if we were conscious that printing and advertising cost a great deal of money. If a designer could pretend that the money to be spent to reproduce his design was his own, I suspect he would subject himself to far more rigid disciplines.

When he examines his work with relation to its function,

THE CORONATION OF POPE JOHN XXIII

Today television will bring the coronation of a new Pope within the sight of more people than have witnessed all the coronations in the history of the Papacy ◉ As the solemn and majestic ceremonies unfold before a massed crowd of 600,000 in St. Peter's Square, Eurovision cameras will broadcast the event over an international network to some 30 million television viewers in seven European nations ◉ To enable millions of Americans to see the ceremonies the CBS Television Network will present an hour-long nationwide broadcast highlighting the principal features of the event ◉ Recorded on video tape directly from the Eurovision broadcast, and edited in London with on-the-scene commentary by CBS News Correspondent Winston Burdett, it will be flown by jet plane to America for broadcast immediately following tonight's election coverage by CBS News ◉ It will be repeated tomorrow from 10 to 11 am ◉ Be sure to see this historic broadcast on the CBS Television Network ◉ Channel 2

*Diverse themes are unified
by insistence on clarity and originality.*

*A newspaper ad:
John Groth draws an ancient ritual
with sketchy accuracy...*

*A newspaper ad:
Lively photograph depicts
the exuberance of a musical...*

*A trade ad:
Joseph Hirsch conveys
Marian Anderson's intensity...*

*A case cover for two books:
The power of type
to state a message...*

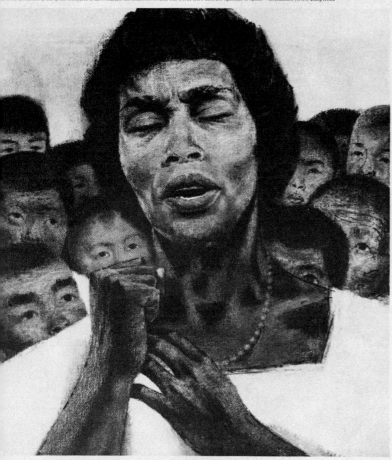

WER TO COMMUNICATE

are on television tonight because we want our fellow
mericans to know what we do. We also want the
merican people to know what one woman accomplished
the field of human communications..."

th this introduction by International Telephone and
egraph Corporation, an extraordinary woman and a
nt corporation each demonstrated more forcefully
n ever before the exceptional ability they share in
mon—their unparalleled power to communicate.

It was a unique experience for millions of Americans
whose hearts like those of millions of Asians were
captured by the spirit and humanity of a great artist
winning new friends for our country.

It was a unique experience, too, for IT&T which for the
first time used a powerful mass communications medium
to describe its own vital world-wide achievements
in communication—and in 60 glowing minutes earned
the gratitude of millions of new friends at home.

But for an increasing number of American industrial
advertisers, television's power to communicate is no new
experience. They are acutely sensitive to its capacity
to convey information with an impact, a reality and a
persuasiveness unmatched by any other medium of mass
communications in all history.

And year after year, the television network that provides
the largest audiences for industry is CBS Television
where such outstanding corporations as DuPont, General
Electric, Monsanto, U. S. Steel, Westinghouse, and now
IT&T give their fellow Americans the most significant
picture of industry's role in the life of the nation.

CBS TELEVISION ◉

YEARS
OF
CRISIS
WHERE
WE
STAND

CBS TELEVISION

BEST TELEPLAY WRITING, HOUR OR MORE:
Rod Serling for *The Comedian*
Playhouse 90

BEST DRAMATIC SERIES WITH CONTINUING CHARACTERS:
Gunsmoke

BEST LIVE CAMERA WORK, THE ENTIRE SERIES:
Playhouse 90

BEST COMEDY SERIES:
The Phil Silvers Show

BEST EDITING OF A FILM FOR TELEVISION:
Mike Pozen for *How To Kill a Woman*
Gunsmoke

BEST SINGLE PERFORMANCE BY ACTRESS:
Polly Bergen on *Helen Morgan Story*
Playhouse 90

BEST CINEMATOGRAPHY FOR TELEVISION:
Harold E. Wellman, *Hemo the Magnificent*
Bell Telephone Science Series

BEST NEW PROGRAM SERIES OF YEAR:
Seven Lively Arts

FIRST "SPECIAL TRUSTEE" AWARD:
Jack Benny
on *The Jack Benny Show*

BEST SINGLE PROGRAM OF YEAR:
The Comedian
on *Playhouse 90*

BEST CONTINUING PERFORMANCE, MALE, PERSON WHO PLAYS HIMSELF:
Jack Benny on *The Jack Benny Show*

BEST COMEDY WRITING:
Nat Hiken, Billy Friedberg, Phil Sharp, Terry Ryan, Coleman Jacoby, Arnold Rosen, Sidney Zelinka, A. J. Russell and Tony Webster
The Phil Silvers Show

BEST TELEPLAY WRITING, HALF-HOUR OR LESS:
Paul Monash for *The Lonely Wizard*
Schlitz Playhouse of Stars

BEST COVERAGE OF UNSCHEDULED NEWSWORTHY EVENT: Feb. 3, Rikers Island (N.Y.) plane crash on *World News Roundup*

BEST DIRECTION, HALF-HOUR OR LESS:
Robert Stevens, *The Glass Eye*
Alfred Hitchcock Presents

BEST NEWS COMMENTARY:
Edward R. Murrow
for *See It Now*

BEST DRAMATIC ANTHOLOGY SERIES:
Playhouse 90

Thanks
—for giving your best!

Last week the talented and creative people who attracting to television the largest audiences in th history of show business honored the outstanding achievements of a number of their colleagues. That so many were able to do their best work on

THE CBS TELEVISION NETWORK

helps explain why this network was able to win largest average nighttime audiences in each of th 66 consecutive Nielsen Reports since July 1955.

*The "Emmy" award-winners
are featured in this trade advertisement,
using the year's "eye" ads in a new layout.*

*A 36-page book features the success
of the dramatic "Playhouse 90" series—
a "long shot" that paid off!*

he wouldn't bury the text and render it illegible on the ground that it is inferior anyway. He will insist, instead, that it be better. If no one will write a better text, he will have to learn to write it himself. For having become, in effect, his own client, he will want to be sure that what he has to say will be clearly understood—that this is his primary function.

He will find that the most satisfying solutions to a graphic problem come from its basic content. He will find it unnecessary and offensive to superimpose a visual effect on an unrelated message.

He might even find that writers, too, have a certain skill, and he might enjoy reading them, and making their work legible.

Perhaps the most important thing that would happen is that all those pointless questions about tradition and modernism, whether our typography is American or European, will become properly irrelevant. All of these influences, and many more, will have become part of the designer's total design vocabulary.

If he applies it successfully, the end product will show no traces of having been designed at all. It will look perfectly obvious and inevitable.

If he is more concerned with how well his job is done than he is about whether or not it is "new," he will even win awards for his performance.

But no matter how many honors are bestowed on him throughout his career, he will never mistake the printed page for an art gallery.

At your conference last year, the most stimulating speaker for me, was not a designer at all. He was a semanticist—Dr. Anatol Rapoport of the University of Michigan's Mental Health Research Institute. In trying to analyze our profes-

Johnson's whole ball of wax is on the CBS Television Network

Starting this Fall, S. C. Johnson will concentrate all of its network television advertising on the network which repeatedly delivers the largest nationwide audiences in advertising.

As the biggest manufacturer of wax polishes in the world, Johnson needs the biggest audiences it can get—and has found them consistently on the CBS Television Network.

For the past three years it has demonstrated the efficiency of its products to an average audience of 27 million viewers, aided and abetted by Red Skelton. In its programming plans for the Fall, it has not only announced the renewal of this popular comedy series, but has *increased* its product-exposure by ordering two additional nighttime programs.*

Johnson underwrites its belief in the effectiveness of network television by committing most of its advertising appropriation to a medium still growing at the rate of *600,000 viewers a month*.

This same confidence accounts for the current wave of renewals by America's leading advertisers on the network which in 70 consecutive Nielsen Reports issued since July 1955, has been credited with the largest audiences in all television.

* "T...
"Dick Powell's Zane G...

One of a series of "eye" ads,
announcing the continuation of sponsorship
by major advertisers.

A drawing by Jacob Landau
directs attention
to an important dramatic program

sion, he was pretty close, I think, when he thought of us as intermediaries. He likened us to performers. Actors who speak other people's lines. Musicians who interpret what composers write.

Though he plucked us from the stratosphere and put us in our proper place, he also soothed our ruffled egos by gently suggesting that some performances could be superb.

To the extent that his analysis is correct, it might be useful to quote an old "square" writer on the subject.

I happen at the moment to be working on a reprint of *Hamlet*. Here is what the author demanded of performers:

"Speak the speech, I pray you, as I pronounce it to you... For if you mouth it, as many of your players do, I would as lief the town crier spoke my lines.

"Nor do not saw the air too much with your hand, thus; but use all gently. For in the very torrent, tempest, and as I may say, whirlwind of your passion, you must acquire and beget a temperance that may give it smoothness.

"Be not too tame, neither. Suit the action to the word, the word to the action... For anything so overdone is from the purpose of playing, whose end is, to hold, as 'twere, the mirror up to nature.

"And let those who play your clowns speak no more than is set down for them. Go make you ready."

REMEMBER?

FACE OF CRIME—20TH CENTURY

MURROW INTERVIEWS TRUMAN

CHURCHILL, MAN OF THE CENTURY

MAN IN SPACE—CONQUEST

INTERVIEW WITH TITO

ALGERIA AFLAME

MISSILE DEVELOPMENT

MARIAN ANDERSON—SEE IT NOW

KHRUSHCHEV—FACE THE NATION

GENERAL GAVIN—WHERE WE STAND

DR. TELLER—GREAT CHALLENGE

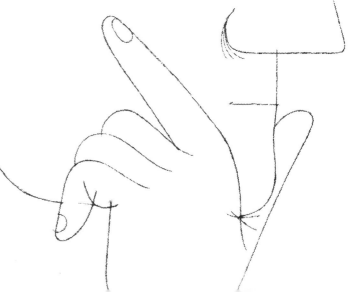

*Full-page newspaper advertisement,
with a drawing by Kurt Weihs,
sums up a year's special news programs.*

*A typical spread of the annual CBS diary (1958)
illustrated by Carl Erickson*

TONIGHT AT 6 ON CHANNEL 2

"Man of the Century"
a full-hour dramatic summary of the career of
Sir Winston Churchill, the first production on
"The Twentieth Century"
a new weekly series of brilliant documentary
reports depicting the world-shaking events and
towering personalities that are shaping our era.

A CBS TELEVISION PREMIERE

*The British artist-journalist,
Feliks Topolski, was commissioned
to paint Churchill
for a newspaper advertisement
announcing a new series*

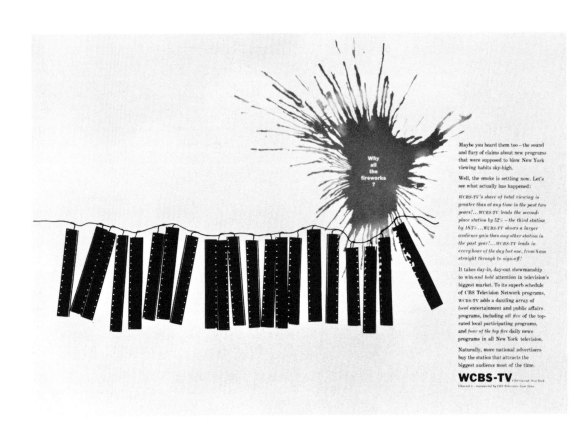

*New programs on a local television station
are dramatized in this trade ad.*

*Two drawings by Ben Shahn
illustrate completely different program types:
a drama and a documentary*

PLAYHOUSE 90

Television's distinguished 90 minute weekly dramatic program opens a brilliant new season with the thrilling story of Spain's greatest bullfighter

THE DEATH OF MANOLETE
starring JACK PALANCE
SUZY PARKER
Produced by Martin Manulis in Television City
9:30 TONIGHT
live over the CBS Television Network ⑤
ON CHANNEL 2

SEE IT NOW brings you a report on Puerto Rico's dramatic efforts to raise her living standards, and surveys the various problems caused by the mass migration of her people to the United States. See

The Puerto Ricans
—AMERICANS ON THE MOVE

Produced in Puerto Rico and New York by Edward R. Murrow and Fred W. Friendly. Broadcast over The CBS Television Network

TODAY AT 5 ON CHANNEL 2

ties. Bath room little used. Telephone. Near Underground. £3 15s.—Wes. 0664.

ANYONE POSSESSING INFORMATION

about the case of Rees Mathry, an innocent man convicted of murder, please contact Paul Mathry at 611 River Street.

DISTRESSED GENTLEFOLK'S AID ASSOCIATION appeals for widow of professional

man, aged 77, living alone, fractured spine and

The cover of a kit containing
ads, films and slides for a dramatic program
is designed to create immediate curiosity
about the program.

The sun-and-eye theme appears in a trade announcement
and in a promotion piece
for daytime programs

THE BIG PUSH

THIS SUMMER America's consumers wil[l]
fill their shopping baskets fuller than a[ny]
summer in their history. And they wil[l]
them with the products they know bes[t]
the brands they see on television.

Last summer they spent nearly 10 per [cent]
more than they did the previous winte[r]
7 per cent more for food; 12 per cent m[ore]
for household appliances; 15 per cent m[ore]
in department stores and nearly 8 per [cent]
more on installment purchases.

For the television advertiser, each sum[mer]
becomes more inviting than the last.

Each summer the average family spen[ds]
more time watching television.

Each day 8,000 new families join the v[ast]
television audience, and by July the nu[mber]
of television homes in the country will
total 40,300,000 — nearly 3½ million mo[re]
than last July.

And each summer CBS Television brin[gs]
to its advertisers bigger audiences tha[n]
the summer before and larger than an[y]
other network.

CBS Television advertisers are better
prepared for the big summer sales push
than ever — in fact, this summer 14 per [cent]
more of our winter advertisers will be o[n]
the air than a year ago.

These are compelling facts for an adver[tiser]
who is debating when or where to laun[ch]
his new advertising campaign.

Clearly the time to start is now; the pl[ace]

CBS TELEVISIO[N]

A network ad demonstrates the value of summer program sponsorship

The single column strip
is typical "stack" ad of one evening's programs.

A trade ad features a success story
of spot television announcements

Newsfilm tells the world...

Newsfilm is global not only in its coverage of news, but also in its distribution. There are subscriber stations around the world. In England, Denmark, Holland and Luxembourg. In Australia and Japan. In Hawaii and Alaska. In Canada, Cuba, Mexico and Argentina.

There are three basic reasons for *Newsfilm's* worldwide growth. Its news coverage is fast, professional, complete. It is a product of CBS News, known the world over as broadcasting's finest newsgathering organization. And third, *Newsfilm* is the *only* news service produced especially and exclusively for the use of television stations.

One major subscriber to this service is Independent Television News Limited, the network news service for Great Britain's commercial television system. According to Editor Geoffrey Cox of ITN: "*Newsfilm* has been of immense value to us. We have been able to rely on it with complete confidence as the foundation of our foreign coverage...not only in the United States but throughout the rest of the world. Particularly, *Newsfilm's* reporting of major happenings has been outstanding."

A word to the worldly-wise: *Newsfilm* is available to *all stations*, at home and abroad. Get complete information from...

CBS TELEVISION FILM SALES, INC.

"...the best film programs for all stations"

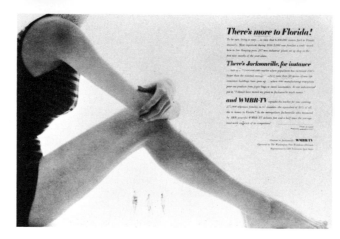

There's _more_ to Florida...

Almost everything in Florida — from its fauna and flora to its economic outlook — is _different_. It's the only state with above-average indexes for all major cities (Sales Management High Spot Cities, May)...and within Florida the _Highest_ Spot City is Jacksonville. Retail sales here are running about five million dollars a month ahead of 1957, and January-April bank clearings were more than nine million dollars ahead of the same period last year.

There's _more_ to WMBR-TV! _In this economic paradise, WMBR-TV maintains its audience lead by wide margins. Consider, for example, local news programming. WMBR-TV's 8:45 am News has a 206% lead over the competition. The One O'Clock Report beats competing news by 265%. WMBR-TV's 6:30 pm News commands a 38.5 rating and a 285% lead over competing news. And its Eleven O'Clock Report smothers the competition's news with a 663% lead. In news as in everything else, it's no news that there's much, much more to..._

Channel 4, Jacksonville · **WMBR-TV**
An Affiliate of the CBS Television Network
Operated by The Washington Post Broadcast Division
Represented by CBS Television Spot Sales

Source: Latest ARB

watch closely!

Television's incredible statistics can be even more bewildering in this record year—if you don't watch them very carefully all the time.

Take the question of measuring* a program's popularity. Do you count the *total audience*—the number of people who tune in during the course of a program (*including* those who tune out after sampling it), or do you measure the *average audience* —the number of people who watch it during the average minute?

Without a single family changing a minute of its viewing behavior you can arrive at a surprisingly different set of figures.

The *total audience*** measurement can produce the most astronomical numbers. But the *average audience* concept has far greater value for a sponsor. Because it is a much more accurate index of the number of people who have seen an advertising message, it has clearly gained more acceptance in the industry.

The clearest single fact about t[...] 1955-56 television season to dat[...] that on an *average audience* ba[...] CBS Television broadcast 7 of t[...] most popular programs at nigh[...] 8 of the top 10 in the daytime.

Moreover, its average program [...] a 12% larger rating at night an[...] a 64% larger rating during the [...] than the second ranking netwo[...]

A record that continues to esta[...] **CBS TELEVISION** as th[...] world's largest advertising me[...]

*All data based on NTI Averages: October '55-Ap[...]

**On this basis too, CBS Television comes out ahe[...] with 6 of the top 10 nighttime programs, 8 of th[...] daytime programs, and averages both day and n[...] 1 million more viewers than the second ranking [...]

48

"THE SECRET LIFE OF DANNY KAYE"

is an unforgettable experience marking a most unusual television debut in behalf of the United Nations International Children's Emergency Fund. Today you will follow the joyful trail of Danny Kaye at his best as he entertains the children of Italy, Greece, Yugoslavia, Switzerland, Turkey, Nigeria, Spain, Morocco, France, England and Israel at the request of UNICEF. For an hour and a half through the cameras of **"SEE IT NOW,"** produced by **EDWARD R. MURROW** and **FRED W. FRIENDLY,** you will see the upturned faces of these children transfigured with delight as Danny clowns his way into their hearts on this unique program **TODAY AT 5** on **CBS TELEVISION** ⑨ **CHANNEL 2**

A trade ad on different ways of reading audience ratings, with a photographic montage by Arik Nepo.

The drawing by David Stone Martin announces a UNICEF *program*

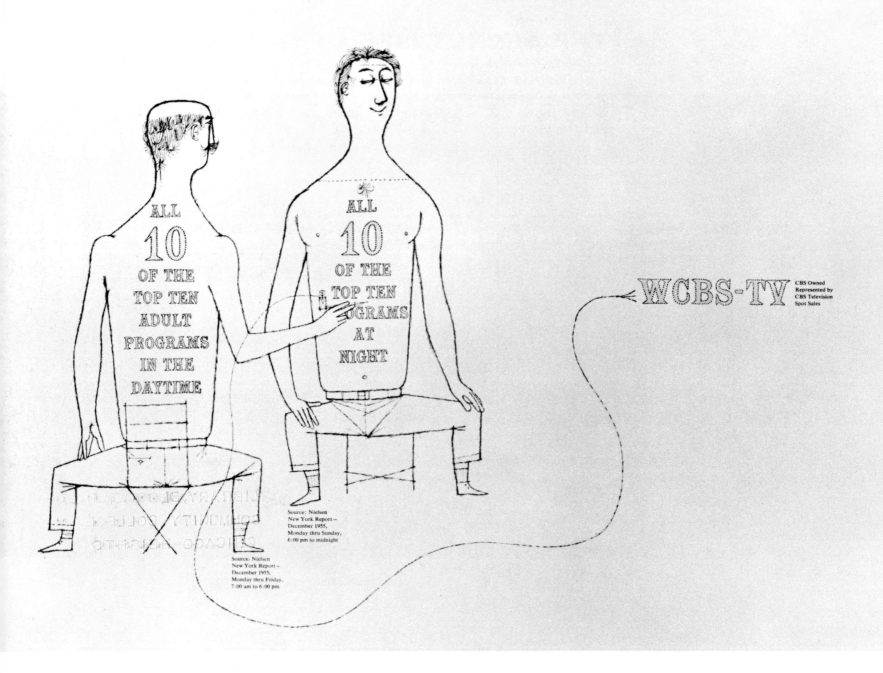

ALL
10
OF THE
TOP TEN
ADULT
PROGRAMS
IN THE
DAYTIME

ALL
10
OF THE
TOP TEN
PROGRAMS
AT
NIGHT

Source: Nielsen
New York Report –
December 1955,
Monday thru Friday,
7:00 am to 6:00 pm

Source: Nielsen
New York Report –
December 1955,
Monday thru Sunday,
6:00 pm to midnight

WCBS-TV

CBS Owned
Represented by
CBS Television
Spot Sales

Contrasting approaches:

Whimsical treatment of a theme for a local television station...
Stark photo for a newspaper ad...
Typographic wit in an ad for a New York station

MR. SUN See this exciting hour-long program
depicts what man has learned about this fiery
of energy and life. In color and black and white

om CBS Television WAAA-TV ◉ **CHANNEL 00**

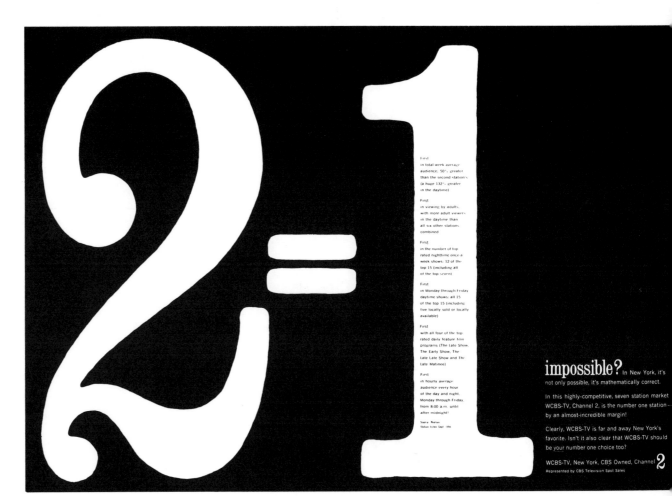

First
in total week average
audience: 50% greater
than the second station's
(a huge 132% greater
in the daytime)

First
in viewing by adults,
with more adult viewers
in the daytime than
all six other stations
combined

First
in the number of top
rated nighttime once a
week shows: 12 of the
top 15 (including all
of the top seven)

First
in Monday through Friday
daytime shows: all 15
of the top 15 (including
five locally sold or locally
available)

First
with all four of the top
rated daily feature film
programs (The Late Show,
The Early Show, The
Late Late Show and The
Late Matinee)

First
in hourly average
audience every hour
of the day and night,
Monday through Friday,
from 8:00 a.m. until
after midnight!

Source: Nielsen
Station Index Sept 1956

impossible? In New York, it's
not only possible, it's mathematically correct.

In this highly-competitive, seven station market
WCBS-TV, Channel 2, is the number one station—
by an almost-incredible margin!

Clearly, WCBS-TV is far and away New York's
favorite. Isn't it also clear that WCBS-TV should
be your number one choice too?

WCBS-TV, New York, CBS Owned, Channel **2**
Represented by CBS Television Spot Sales

The Blue Conventions

Feliks Topolski

major issues of the campaign in a special series of eight half-hour Wednesday night programs entitled "Pick The Winner."

Throughout each week, 2 hours and 20 minutes of the networks eleven scheduled news programs were being devoted primarily to the latest reports on the progress of the candidates and the campaign. In addition, the television audience kept posted on the developing political situation each Sunday afternoon between 5 and 6 with "Face The Nation" and "Bandwagon '56," the network's public affairs programs presenting "live" interviews with the leading spokesmen of both parties together with analyses by CBS News commentators.

Temporarily idle during the two conventions, the 12-man mobile unit of the CBS News Campaign Cavalcade resumed its hot pursuit of Democratic and Republican candidates as they sped across the country appealing for the support of the voters.

Adhering to its practice of previous years the network arranged to provide the fastest and most complete coverage of the election by re-assembling the same team of CBS News reporters and analysts who covered the conventions. In 1952 television's

Cover and sample pages
of a 48-page report
on the television coverage
of the 1956 political conventions,
illustrated by Feliks Topolski

53

*To reproduce faithfully
the pen-ink-pencil-wash techniques
of Feliks Topolski,
the "Blue Conventions" book was printed
in four colors on blue-gray paper*

Each party allocated an afternoon to "Ladies' Day" during which various women high in the party councils addressed the delegates. At the Democratic "Ladies' Day" session Governor Frank Clement, Democratic keynoter, announced: "I don't know how many people are now watching television, but they are probably all women, and I know they will be interested in seeing the pleasant proceedings that are now about to take place."

Both parties held stop watches on the floor demonstrations and called time on their speakers.

At the outset of the Democratic proceedings, Permanent Chairman Sam Rayburn announced that all demonstrations would be restricted to 25 minutes and seconding speeches to 5 minutes each.

Republican Chairman Joseph Martin acted similarly, confining the seconding speeches for the Vice Presidential nomination to 2 minutes. Although these restrictions were not uniformly observed, the speeches were generally held within their time limits. The demonstration following Governor Stevenson's nomination exceeded its prescribed limit by 2½ minutes. Observing the principle of "equal time and treatment," Rayburn permitted the Harriman

STEVENSON

STEVENSON 1872
JOHNSON
DAVIS
HARRY
CHA.

ESTES
for
V. PRESIDENT

Nomination by Acclamation

a progress
report
on
Captain
Kangaroo

CBS TELEVISION CLIENTS & PROGRAMS
April 1956

SEE IT NOW
WITH EDWARD R. MURROW
PRESENTS

REPORT FROM AFRICA

THE PICTURE OF
A CONTINENT'S STRUGGLE
FOR FREEDOM
PART 1: APRIL 23, 1956
PART 2: MAY 17, 1956
FROM 10 TO 11 PM, CNYT
SPONSORED BY
SHULTON, INC. ON
CBS TELEVISION

SEE THESE GREAT PERFORMERS
IN PERSON CELEBRATE
THE 8th ANNIVERSARY OF
THE ED SULLIVAN SHOW

KATE SMITH
LUCILLE BALL AND DESI ARNAZ
GREGORY PECK
RED SKELTON
MARGE AND GOWER CHAMPION
HARRY BELAFONTE
SUSAN HAYWARD
JAMES MASON
RISE STEVENS
EDDIE CANTOR
EDWARD G. ROBINSON
RHONDA FLEMING
ABBOTT AND COSTELLO
ERNEST BORGNINE
VIRGINIA MAYO
CATHY AND BOB CROSBY
JACK PAAR
TERESA BREWER
TAB HUNTER
ROBERT STACK
JOHN DALY
SAM LEVENSON
RUTH GORDON
TEX AND JINX McCRARY
MICHAEL O'SHEA
JEANNE CRAIN
LOUIS ARMSTRONG
RICHARD WIDMARK
RONALD REAGAN
WALTER BRENNAN
WILL ROGERS, JR.
IDA LUPINO
HOWARD DUFF

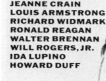

TONIGHT AT 8 CHANNEL 2 CBS TELEVISION

EGYPT-
ISRAEL

SEE IT NOW PRESENTS A SPECIAL HOUR-AND-A-HALF REPORT ON THE CRISIS IN THE MIDDLE EAST WITH EDWARD R. MURROW
AND HOWARD K. SMITH, TUESDAY EVENING, MARCH 13, 1956, FROM 8:30 TO 10:00 PM, CNYT, ON THE CBS TELEVISION NETWORK

All in a day's work:

*Children's morning program
—a presentation.
Report on a continent
—a promotion kit cover.
Folksy morning commentator
—cover for a program booklet.
Evening entertainment
—a newspaper ad.
Mid-East program promotion kit cover*

(The nature of communication provided the theme for the Ninth International Design Conference held in Aspen, Colorado, June 21-27, 1959 which was attended by an outstanding group of international scholars and designers. These included the noted microphotographer, Dr. Roman Vishniac; Prof. Lancelot Hogben, the distinguished mathematician; Prof. S. I. Hayakawa, the eminent semanticist; and the well known British scientist and industrialist, L. L. Whyte. Mr. Golden was among the American designers invited to present papers before the Conference and to take part in the closing panel discussion. The text of his paper as well as excerpts from his remarks on the panel follow.)

Visual environment of advertising

I happen to believe that the visual environment of advertising improves each time a designer produces a good design—*and in no other way.*

There may, indeed, be some cause for concern about the chaos the designer is bringing to the visual environment of advertising.

I think we tend to do this each time we leave our work for the lecture platform or the typewriter. We tend to overstate our case in the most complicated manner, and to confuse the simple purpose of our perfectly honest, useful, little craft with the language of the sociologist, the psychiatrist, the scientist, the art critic, and sometimes even the mystic.

The obvious function of a designer is to design. His principal talent is to make a simple order out of many elements. The very act of designing exposes elements that are inconsistent and must obviously be rejected. When he is in control of these elements he can usually produce an acceptable design. When

A Conversation with
Dr. J. Robert Oppenheimer
Director, Institute for Advanced Study, Princeton, N.J.

Tonight on "See It Now"
edited by Edward R. Murrow and Fred W. Friendly
10:30 on channel 2

BACK TONIGHT

JACK BENNY

7:30 PM, CHANNEL **2** CBS TELEVISION ◉

originating *live* from Television City, Hollywood

Drama and humor of a time:

The simplicity
of a photographic document...
The polished elegance
of a René Bouché portrait

someone else controls them the best he can produce is a counterfeit. This is why at some stage of his maturity he feels the need to have a voice in the content itself. If the advertising designer begins to "examine the purposes to which this vast communications machinery is put" (as a prospectus for this conference suggests), he can run headlong into his basic conflict with the business world—a dissatisfaction with the content he is asked to transmit.

For Business the question of content is very simple. Its objective is reflected in its most important single printed document —the Annual Report. This is the yardstick by which all its decisions are measured. If the Report is unfavorable for very long the business will cease to exist. Whatever contributes to its success is right. Whatever endangers the financial statement is wrong.

Thus the morality of Business is clear and reasonably defensible. The morality of the businessman may be something else again, but as Business gets bigger and bigger, his morality is less and less operative. The man himself tends to disappear and in his place the Corporation Executive begins to emerge.

His first responsibility is to the Corporation and not to society. He would say that in our economy what is right for the corporation must inevitably be good for society, because the successful corporation provides more employment, more products and services, and higher tax payments which pay for still more social services. So without having to make a single social decision the corporation executive can tend strictly to business with the comforting assurance that no matter how it is conducted (short of public scandal), his energies will be socially useful—if the business is sufficiently profitable.

Last Saturday night CBS Television presented the <u>second</u>* most popular hour-and-a-half program of the season, "The Caine Mutiny Court-Martial"... and brought into still sharper focus the picture of CBS Television as America's favorite source of exciting entertainment.

*CBS Television broadcast the <u>most</u> popular 90-minute show of the season—another Ford Star Jubilee program "The Judy Garland Show."

Anybody
here
you don't
know?

Overnight fame
for anonymous people:
A double-page trade ad
on a popular quiz program

The dilemma of the literate advertising designer is that emotionally he is part small businessman and part artist. He isn't strong enough to cut himself off from the world of business to make the personal statement of the artist. He isn't a pure enough businessman to turn his attention completely away from the arts.

He somehow wants the best of both worlds. He becomes a kind of soft-boiled businessman.

When he turns to Business he is told that the content of our time is The Fact. The Fact of Science. The Fact of Business. The Fact is beyond suspicion. It has no views on Art, Religion or Politics. It is not subject to anyone's opinion. It can be measured and tabulated. It is non-controversial.

In an era of mass-marketing, controversy is assumed to be bad for business, for no potential consumer must be offended. Though Business may have no legitimate interest in people, it has an abiding interest in consumers.

The designer for the most part would be willing, I think, to accept The Fact as the content for his work. But he soon discovers that despite the prattle of the public relations expert about "lean, hard facts," the designer is seldom called upon to work with them.

For Business wants him to help create an attitude about the facts, not to communicate them. And only about some of the facts. For facts in certain juxtapositions can offend some portion of the market.

So he finds himself working with half-truths, and feels that he is not using all his talents. He finds that he is part of a gigantic merchandising apparatus in which the media of mass communication have reached a miraculous degree of technical perfection and are being operated at full speed to say as little as necessary in the most impressive way.

The importance of public office
is emphasized by the documentary styling
of a brochure
(containing script and film clips)
and a promotion kit cover

And this, too, is what the advertising designer is called upon to do. If he can adjust himself easily to this framework he can work very happily, and may even be handsomely rewarded for his efforts.

If he is reluctant to accept the role of a propagandist for business, but looks further for a deeper meaning for his work, he might find greater solace on the psychiatrist's couch than he will in Aspen.

There is one inviting avenue of escape that seems to give comfort to an increasing number of designers, and certainly to almost all the younger ones. It is that wonderful panacea that came to full flower in a disturbed postwar world: the abstract expressionist school of painting. It is in itself a Fact. It is acceptable because it is Art.

Business can accept it because it is successful, and oddly enough "safe" since it says absolutely nothing. The cynical advertising designer can embrace it because it can help him demonstrate his independence of content. The young designer finds it a wonderful shortcut—a do-it-yourself Art. And anyone can find delight in its total concentration on technique.

But I doubt the necessity to search in so many fruitless directions for a solution to the designer's plight.

Once he stops confusing Art with design for Business and stops making demands on the business world that it has neither the capacity nor the obligation to fulfill, he'll probably be all right. In fact I think he is pretty lucky. In the brave new world of Strontium 90—a world in which craftsmanship is an intolerable deterrent to mass production—it is a good thing to be able to practice a useful craft.

It is a craft that is susceptible to further growth and that can so far do something that neither the Management Execu-

Harvest

*Cover of a folder
and a
double-page advertisement
with drawings by
Ben Shahn*

Harvest

Each year America's rooftops yield a new harvest—a vast aluminum garden spreading increasingly over the face of the nation.

The past season produced a bumper crop on all counts: 3½ million new antennas bringing the total number of television homes to 34,567,000.

The average television family spent more time watching its screen than ever—*5 hours and 20 minutes a day.*

Day and night CBS Television broadcast the majority of the most popular programs and during the past season extended its popularity by enlarging the network to 209 stations—a 75% increase in a year.

Today CBS Television delivers more homes for less money than any other network, and in comparison with its closest competitor, offers an even better buy than it did a year ago.

CBS Television advertisers invested $165,268,000 over the past 12 months—a 20% greater investment than was made on any other network.

By demonstrating television's ability to move our expanding national product into the American home *most efficiently,* CBS Television has become the world's largest single advertising medium.

THE CBS TELEVISION NETWORK

after you...

It was pretty nice of the ABC Television Network to salute its fellow networks in a recent advertisement for their program awards from the Academy of Television Arts and Sciences.

We had intended doing the same kind of thing earlier this season when they launched some very exciting program ideas.

But they beat us to it—just as they beat us to *Disneyland*.

When competing networks applaud each other the applause is genuine; for each success is a fresh demonstration of the value of network television to the audience and the advertiser.

Only through network television can 65 million people share simultaneously the pleasure of NBC's memorable *Peter Pan* ...or discover a great comic like George Gobel.

Only through network television can an advertiser reach 41 million people each week as economically, for example, as he can on *I Love Lucy*—another network developed program.

The steady improvement of television is due not so much to the enormous investment of money, time and effort as it is to the constant goad of network competition.

This is the heart of the American system of broadcasting. This is why television builds larger audiences each year.

And this is what has made television in America the world's largest advertising medium.

The CBS Television Network

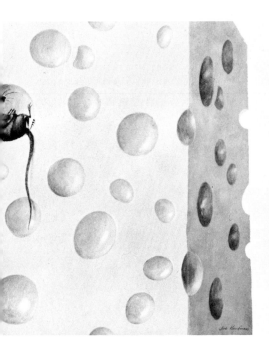

*Ludwig Bemelmans
illustrates a network announcement.*

*Joe Kaufman's drawing
promotes local sales of television time*

tive nor the electronic computer can do.

If he doesn't like the end his craft serves, he can probably find a client whose products or services seem worthwhile. He can "improve the visual environment of advertising" by a flat refusal to do bad work for anyone, and thus maintain the standards of his craft.

He can take pleasure in the fact that the performance of his colleagues in graphic design is improving all the time.

He can even take pleasure, as I do, in the fact that a number of designers are beginning to watch their language.

Maybe they realized that we were beginning to frighten our clients by our strange literature. (After all, it wasn't very long ago that clients were suspicious of any advertising design that merely looked handsome.) Maybe they are finding work more rewarding than talking about it. But whatever the reason, I think (and hope) that there is a detectable change in the climate which once produced the young man who wanted to change the course of the graphic arts.

Even Leo Lionni has become weary of his preposterous invention of the New Renaissance Man, and is ready to embrace anyone who can do one thing well rather than many things badly.

Will Burtin has announced that he just doesn't care whether or not typography is an Art, so long as it does what it is supposed to do.

Saul Bass had admitted that "our typographic designs are . . . ridiculously small expressions of a profound cultural pattern."

Even this present conference concedes that the only way to demonstrate the process of communication "by Image" is by visual exhibit.

It may be useful, however, to reconsider this simplest, most

TARGET In 1955 CBS Television achieved a nine-year objective: delivering the most popular programs to the largest audience at the lowest cost in all television.

A variation of the trademark becomes the illustration of the theme

"what's Steel doing?"

TONIGHT The United States Steel Corporation moves its distinguished television program "The United States Steel Hour" to CBS Television.

Some of the reasons for this move may be found in the achievements of the CBS Television Network during the past season:

CBS Television broadcast a majority of the most popular programs – day and night...

CBS Television continued to deliver more homes for less money than any other network...and in comparison with its nearest competitor offers an even better buy today than it did a year ago...

CBS Television advertisers invested $165,265,000 over the past twelve months – 20% more than was invested on the second ranking network...

During the past season more families reserved more time for television than for any other form of mass communication – a daily average of 5 hours and 20 minutes in television homes now numbering 34,567,000. And among all mass communications CBS Television continued to maintain its position as the world's largest single advertising medium.

Thus it is not surprising that the American corporation whose activity has traditionally been regarded as an index of the nation's economic health should choose CBS Television to register its impact on American life.

CBS TELEVISION

valid, of our group activities. We have annual competitions in which we give each other awards and, by demonstration, set standards for our craft.

This is a sincere but disconcerting activity of perhaps questionable value since the criteria of these exhibitions are usually so poorly defined. Their purpose is to impress and to educate the business community and to honor practitioners in our field.

Yet, who hasn't heard the familiar client refrain: "I don't want an ad that will win a medal. I want one that sells." And who among us hasn't said with some embarrassment, "Sure it's nice to get a medal, but they gave it to me for the wrong job." Obviously we aren't talking to each other very clearly in our exhibitions either.

Let me try to summarize my own experiences as a juror.

In a relatively small regional show the generous jury found no more than 30 pieces they thought were worth hanging— and only two that seemed to merit recognition. The exhibition committee was aghast. They instructed the jury to hang a predetermined quota of 80 and to award 12 prizes. The jury was thus forced to give its endorsement to pieces which in their opinion had no merit whatever, and an incompetent piece of work could thereafter be cited as having set a standard.

In another regional show the jury awarded 9 of 10 prizes to a single man. He was clearly brilliant in every category. The exhibition committee explained that it was not only "unfair" to the others, but that it would so alienate the other local advertising agencies that they would boycott future competitions. The brilliant young man was awarded 2 prizes.

In a large exhibition with a large jury "democratically rep-

For insertion Saturday, September 10, 1955
3 cols. x 240 lines = 720 lines
Position Request: Television Listings page.

CBS Television presents the premiere tonight of an
adult and provocative dramatic series of the old West

GUNSMOKE

starring James Arness

Hailed by critics as the "High Noon" of broadcasting
when it first excited millions on radio, you are certain
to be caught up in the tension which hangs over a
sun-baked frontier community, and to applaud a new
star on television. **Tonight at 10, channel 2**

For insertion Tuesday, September 20, 1955
4 cols. x 600 lines = 400 lines
Position Request: Television Listings page.

Premiere tonight! **NAVY LOG**

Don't miss "THE FROGMEN," the gripping story of courage by a
Navy underwater demolition team. It is the opening program
in a new adventure series based on the factual record of heroism
performed by U. S. Navy personnel aboard ships, planes
and submarines, and produced in cooperation
with the United States Navy
Tonight at 8:00 on channel **2**

THREE PREMIERES TONIGHT: Navy Log: 8:00...You'll Never Get Rich: 8:30...Joe and Mabel 9:00

⊙ *premiere tonight!*

Robin Hood

starring Richard Greene
and Bernadette O'Farrell

Actually filmed in Sherwood
Forest, the classic story
of the famous outlaw who roamed
the English countryside as the
protector of the poor and defender
of the weak comes to life tonight
on CBS Television with Richard
Greene starring in the title role.

Tonight at 7:30
channel **2**

CBS TELEVISION

FORD STAR JUBILEE
presents
JUDY
GARLAND
with special guest star
DAVID
WAYNE

— the first of a once-a-month series of
brilliant hour-and-a-half programs. Be sure
to see Judy for the first time on television
singing the songs that have endeared
her to millions and bringing a new peak of
enjoyment to the television audience.

9:30 TONIGHT

CBS Television, channel **2**
*a live program broadcast in black-and-white
and color from Television City*

1 3 4 5 6 7 8 9 10 12 19

Premiere tonight!

One of the top comedians
of Broadway and Hollywood,
Phil Silvers, in the role of
a top sergeant, brings to your
screen a running and hilarious
picture of army camp life;
its trials, tribulations, snafus and
surprises. Up to his neck in dubious
enterprises, Phil Silvers offers a half-
hour of side-splitting entertainment.

starring **Phil Silvers**

you'll never get rich

Tonight at 8:30 channel **2**

THREE PREMIERES TONIGHT: Navy Log: 8:00 pm...You'll Never Get Rich: 8:30 pm...Joe and Mabel 9:00 pm

GUNSMOKE
starring James Arness

NAVY LOG

you'll never get rich

FORD STAR JUBILEE
JUDY GARLAND
DAVID WAYNE

9:30 TONIGHT
2

Robin Hood
starring Richard Greene
and Bernadene O'Farrell

Tonight at 7:30
channel 2
CBS TELEVISION

"CBS would appear to have a winner"
JACK GOULD, NEW YORK TIMES

"Got off to a fine start"
N.Y. JOURNAL AMERICAN

"Top notch quality... superb photography, realism and pacing..."
ST. LOUIS GLOBE DEMOCRAT

"Will outdraw its Western competition"
N.Y. DAILY NEWS

"The best (of the new candidates)..." TIME MAGAZINE

"Loaded with suspense, full of realism, authentic..." N.Y. HERALD TRIBUNE

"An irresistibly funny television series"
N.Y. HERALD TRIBUNE

"A very funny and well done show... Silvers is a great comedian" NEW YORK POST

"Packed with humor... (Silvers) is superb"
NEW YORK TIMES

"We haven't laughed so much in years... Silvers... will be the comedy standout of the 1955 season"
N.Y. DAILY NEWS

"Perfectly wonderful"
HARRIET VAN HORNE, N.Y. WORLD-TELEGRAM

"Triumphant production"
NEW YORK TIMES

"There's never been anything like the one woman show staged by Judy Garland... over CBS...pure magic. CBS had the best spectacular to date"
HARRIET VAN HORNE, N.Y. WORLD-TELEGRAM

"Will go down as another triumph...an hour-and-a-half of excellent televiewing"
RADIO DAILY

"She proved herself as great a performer on television as in the movies and on the stage"
BEN GROSS, N.Y. DAILY NEWS

"Rousing entertainment ...first rate..." NEW YORK TIMES

"The answer to those who have been crying for entertaining quality shows for youngsters...of interest to old and young alike" N.Y. DAILY NEWS

AS ADVERTISED

The excitement of the critics over the new CBS Television programs was matched by the enthusiasm of the audience. (More people, for example, watched the first "Ford Star Jubilee" than any other 90-minute program on any network in television history. And it was identified with a *single* sponsor!)

To advertisers the real significance of this achievement is that with each program the performance was equal to the promise. For the past four years they have known that CBS Television has delivered more of the most popular programs at a lower cost per thousand than any other television network. Now they can count on CBS Television to enhance its value even further during the coming season.

This confidence is perhaps the underlying reason why American business continues to invest more on CBS Television than on any other single advertising medium in the world. **CBS TELEVISION**

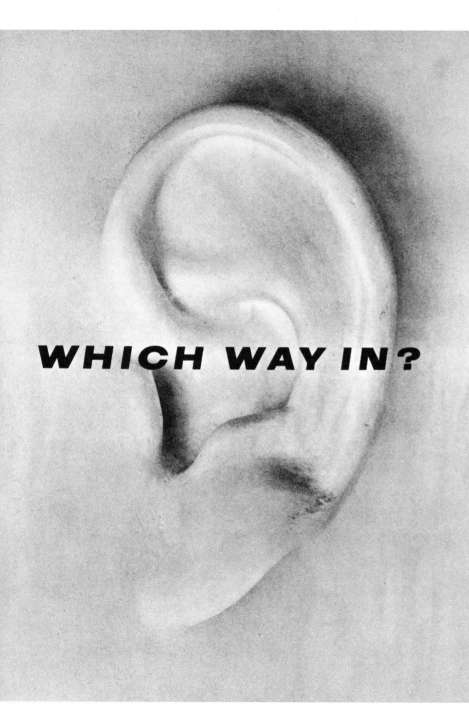

WHICH WAY IN?

How to make the most memorable impression on the human mind is the subject of a now classic debate among the advocates of mass communication media.

It started with the advent of radio and the thesis that the living voice best moved men to action because it could tell your story with human persuasiveness, give it the precise emphasis your message required, and make every line a headline.

The partisans of the printed page have cited arguments as old as Confucius and held that, in addition to the authority of the printed word, the use of pictures could arrest, clarify, evoke a mood and a desire to buy that the spoken word alone could never achieve.

Since the appearance of television, the debate seems somewhat academic. We'd like to participate in it, but nobody wants to listen. For we've never found anyone who doubted television's impact... even before it began.

It was obvious at once that television makes the strongest impression. But it was not so certain to make it with comparable economy.

Yet television already wins larger audiences than any other mass medium. And it already reaches more people per dollar than printed media. To deliver the same total circulation today, television costs half as much as a group of magazines and a quarter as much as a group of newspapers.

And in all television, the network with the lowest cost per thousand is CBS Television —20% lower than the second network.

Advertisers, convinced that the eye and ear work best together, seem to have settled the debate with some finality. In the first quarter of 1954, they made a greater investment in the facilities of CBS Television than in any broadcasting network or national magazine.

CBS TELEVISION

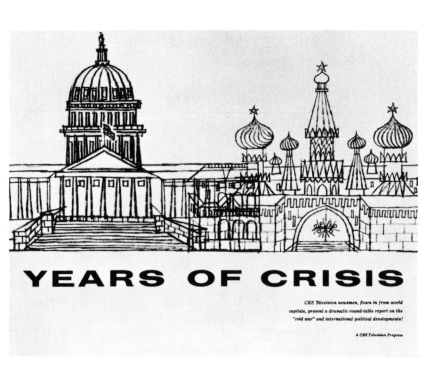

YEARS OF CRISIS

CBS Television newsmen, flown in from world capitals, present a dramatic round-table report on the "cold war" and international political developments!

A CBS Television Program

*Art school props
dramatize the television story
in this trade advertisement.*

*A drawing by Rudi Bass
is used on the cover
of an annual year-end program*

resenting every school of thought" the jury was broken up into small groups—each to judge different categories. The standards of one group were totally at odds with the next and yet its task was to produce a single cohesive exhibition.

I saw the work of an artist eliminated from one category because he had been represented in the last 10 exhibitions and wasn't "new."

In another category he was singled out for special attention by a group which had less interest in novelty than in distinction.

One group was earnestly trying to select a "representative cross-section" of advertising. Another was selecting only those entries which corresponded to their notion of the avant-garde movement.

One refused to hang any part of a large campaign—clearly the best in the show—on the grounds that another single ad in the same series was awarded a prize the year before. Yet another could select the same work in another category because it "continued to maintain the highest standards."

I saw one group reluctantly eliminating work that it admired because their category called for a fixed number of exhibits while another was having trouble finding enough to fill its quota.

On still another occasion the exhibition committee discovered that the jury had failed to find a single example from an industry that was the largest user of advertising in America. This was immediately corrected though nobody before had discovered anything worth hanging.

I have seen jurors sometimes unhappy because memorable work which they had seen in publications never appeared among the exhibition entries. They didn't see how their show could truly reflect the year's accomplishments without the

early returns on THE

M⊙RNING SHOW

It's off to a great start! In its first five days...

It increased sets in use by 39%.*

It won over 45% share of audience.*

It covered areas—including all major markets—with close to 23 million television homes.**

It offered the largest early morning station line

It sold at the lowest over-all price in all televisi

It brought its first sponsor 16,558 replies to a single announcement!

Whether your budget is large or small, you can g big returns on "The Morning Show." Try it once or once a day...once a week...once a month... or as often as you need it.

CBS TELEVISIO

*Trendex, March 15-19.

**With outlets in t Pacific Time Zon through the companion progra "Panorama Pacific

all America has heard him...

An antique weather vane
becomes the symbol for advertisements,
brochures and on-the-air titles
for an early morning program.

The promotion folder for a mystery show
is illustrated by David Stone Martin

missing work, but they were prevented by exhibition practice, from showing it.

I have even known entrants who prayed that the jury wouldn't select more than one of their entries, because they couldn't afford the hanging fee. They had submitted many entries since they couldn't know whether the jury would be "old guard" or "avant-garde."

Perhaps my most puzzling experience as a juror was to serve with a man I had long admired. He had been demonstrating for years that any page in which the hand of the designer was evident was a bad page—that a good concept flawlessly and simply executed should be the objective of every art director.

The category was "Magazine Advertising: Design of complete unit." I had found an ad which consisted of an outstanding photograph and a single line of copy. It didn't seem to be one of those accidental photographs, but a clearly thought out solution to a problem. My co-juror snorted in derision. "This is nothing but a picture and a caption. Where is the 'design'? Anybody can put a caption under a picture. *He hasn't done anything to it.*"

For me the wheel had turned full circle. Now that we had demonstrated how very difficult it was to produce something simple and were beginning to train our clients to understand it, we had to parade our bag of tricks to demonstrate our agility more obviously.

It would be useful, I'm sure, to discuss ways to define our exhibitions more sharply.

Should they be representative or selective? What standards should they reflect? Is it wiser to have large or small juries? Should there be different jurors and different standards from

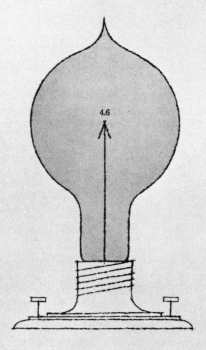

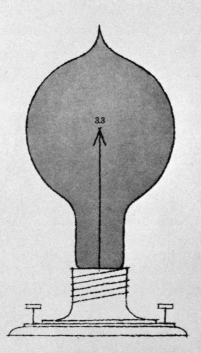

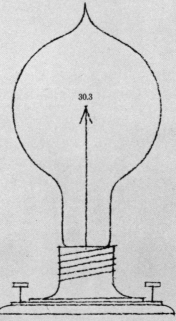

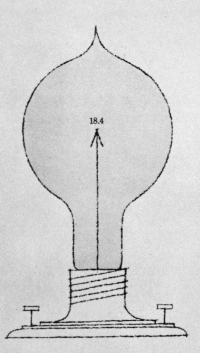

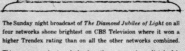

The Sunday night broadcast of *The Diamond Jubilee of Light* on all four networks shone brightest on CBS Television where it won a higher Trendex rating than on all the other networks combined.

This was a surprise to nobody since the program immediately followed CBS Television's *Toast of the Town* which habitually has a higher rating than any other Sunday night program. It simply reaffirmed what every advertiser knows: namely, the tremendous value of surrounding a single program with the strongest possible schedule.

Actually, this experience becomes even less exceptional when you consider the strength of the entire CBS Television schedule. For in the major markets where networks compete—and popularity can be directly compared—the average program on CBS Television, day or night, consistently wins the largest audiences. And wins them at the lowest cost per thousand in network television. **CBS TELEVISION**

     Brightest bulb—highest rating: An electric company's program appearing simultaneously on four networks

Supersalesman

*Trendex, Oct. '53-Mar. '54.

**On the two most recent occasions when sponsored programs were broadcast at the same time over the leading networks, they won a 29%—and a 96%—higher rating on CBS Television.

It's no little trick to make a tentful of people laugh. But it's something else again to get a nation-wide audience laughing—at the same instant.

And laughter, as every salesman knows, is a most effective sales tool. And so are all the other moods an entertainer can evoke. For they help you shift your prospect's interest—willingly—from whatever's on his mind to the product on yours.

This, perhaps, is television's greatest value to an advertiser. It creates a receptive mood in 30 million homes for more than five hours a day. It is always part-entertainer, part-salesman.

This, certainly, is why CBS Television has always made creative programming its most important activity. And why, in the major markets where the networks compete—and popularity can best be compared—CBS Television consistently wins the largest average audience: 11 per cent larger at night, and 27 per cent larger in the daytime.*

Advertisers have found that placing their programs on the most popular network gives them a headstart in ratings**—and a headstart in sales.

That's why their investment on CBS Television for the first quarter was over 45 per cent greater than a year ago. (*And in 1953 it was the greatest in broadcasting history!*) That's why it's *still* growing.

CBS Television can bring you the most receptive audiences in all America, because it has most of the programs most of your customers want.

CBS TELEVISION

Humor is the subject, a solarized photo is the illustration

Television turns on its power

To an advertiser this must surely seem the most rewarding and exciting season in television's history.

This year for the first time Publishers Information Bureau reports a television network rolling up the largest seven-month total of advertising revenue of any network, magazine or newspaper—over $77 million.

This year television is exploiting all of its complex skills, to make it an even greater catapult to sales.

This year, for example, every television network is exerting its all-out effort to bring the richest possible variety of entertainment to its audience.

Take tonight. On CBS Television you find the first of a brilliant new series entitled "The Best of Broadway," originating from its new modern Color Studio 72. Tonight's broadcast stars Helen Hayes, Claudette Colbert, Fredric March and Charles Coburn in "The Royal Family" —*four* Academy Award winners in a single play.

You also find Arthur Godfrey, one of the cornerstones that form the solid foundation of the CBS Television program schedule—a schedule designed to provide lasting entertainment value *and* lowest cost-per-thousand.

It is this basic design which gives the real clue to why advertisers today are committing more of their investments to CBS Television than to any other single medium.

CBS TELEVISION

year to year? Does the practice of awards encourage a community feeling among designers or contribute to their disunity? Shouldn't an exhibition announce its jury and its criteria *before* entries are submitted rather than wade through a mass of material that seems to have been submitted in error?

Must selections be limited by an exhibitor's ability to pay?

I can't help but feel that if these questions can be fully discussed, and solutions are found for them, there would be fewer and more significant exhibitions. And the advertising designer will have taken a great step forward in improving his visual environment.

---

*Excerpts from the panel discussion
related to William Golden's paper at the
Aspen Design Conference:*

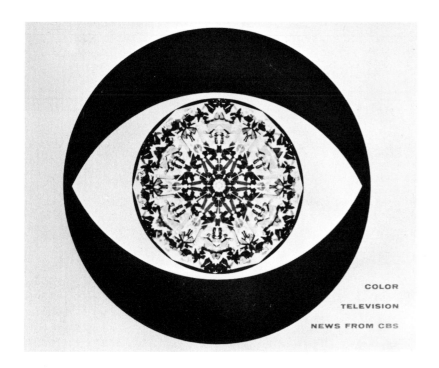

A press kit
for color television

*Q: How would you define the role
of the designer as contrasted
to the role
of the fine artist?*

GOLDEN: I think they're two completely different things. I think all the trouble in this field comes from someone's assumption that they are maybe the same person. I think the fine artist makes a personal statement about his world, and his reactions to his world. He makes it to a limited audience, or to a big audience—but it's all his. He controls every bit of it. The advertising designer has a completely different function. He may be someone who thought he wanted to be a painter—but wasn't. It's a pretty hard thing to be a painter. You have to have an awful lot of guts. But I don't mean to run the designer down. If he's honest enough, he becomes a professional who can do something special. But this something special is for sale—it is communicating something that is not his own. I think the trouble comes when he tries to make it a work of art, too. I think the two are completely different things. I think a lot of designers, who are talented and intelligent don't find this very satisfying. But they're not going to find it more satisfying by pretending it's something it isn't.

Q: Could you expound on the designer's use of the artist?

Coronation Souvenir

GOLDEN: I'll try. I take an advertising problem where I am trying to say something to somebody, and I run through a number of ideas. It seems to me that a particular artist, because I know his work and some of his reactions, might be able to bring more to this particular problem than, let's say, a photographer or a commercial drawing. Now, I myself think it's absolutely useless to go to an artist who has values of his own unless these values coincide with what you're trying to say. Then you present your problem. But you don't tell him — I want a picture of this man, here—this man, there—and so on. This was done during the war in OWI where a lot of fine artists were listed for posters — and they did a big bunch of junk that was never printed. You want what a certain man has—and then you leave him free to do it. You have defined what you hope will happen—but not precisely how he's to do it. I find that most of the time it works. Sometimes it doesn't work, and you simply don't print. You know the artist performed his job in good faith and you pay him. But this is the kind of a gamble you have to take.

There was a very good laboratory set up for this by my wife, Cipe Pineles, when she was art director of *Seventeen*. She thought that a magazine for young people, who were relatively uncorrupted, might not mind fiction being illustrated by painters. And she laid down one rule, which is the only sound one. She said: "The only thing I will accept from you is something you will take back and put in your gallery." This worked very, very well. I think she got the best out of them.

Q: What about the quality of the students and beginners who come to you with their work?

GOLDEN: By and large it's not of great value because it's pretty imitative. Students are apt to say: "We don't copy a Ben Shahn drawing. We try to explore the idiom." They just think they don't copy it. Probably the greatest struggle of all is to find out what you yourself can do particularly well. It doesn't have to be *like* anybody else. But it has to be valid in its own right. This is a pretty tough craft. It takes a lot of hard work. And I think that unless you can get some craft satisfaction in doing it, you're not going to get much else. Craftsmanship is something people have to nourish and hang on to. It's disappearing from our society. I don't care whether you're a shoemaker or a shirtmaker or a typesetter or a printer. Craftsmanship is valuable. I see nothing more rewarding than to try to do something as well as you can.

82

Philip's homage

Meet Mr. Lookit...

He climbed out of our television set and asked for a job. Said he was a Jester. We asked him what he could do.

He said a Jester's business was to amuse his master, to make him laugh, to take his mind off gloomy world affairs, and by his liveliness at meals to assist in his lord's digestion.

Pretty fancy talk, we thought. We told him thanks, but we didn't know anyone these days who could afford to hire a private entertainer.

He said we were missing the point. He'd seen an awful lot of entertainment in the last couple of hundred years and people never had it so good. They had more and better entertainment at the flick of a switch than anybody he ever worked for.

He meant television, of course. But we weren't falling for this obvious buttering-up. Said we'd call him if anything turned up... but not to wait around. We already had most of the most popular programs in town. And after all he was a has-been. Jesters died out long ago. But we might rent his weird get-up for a costume show some time.

He got kind of sore at this. Said he'd been working steady all the time, all over the world. Just using disguises. In the circus, he's the clown; in the movies, he's the slap stick comic; in the ventriloquist act he's the clever repartee (sic)

— the "Dummy"; in the opera, theatre and radio, he used different names. Thought it only right he should be on television. Said he *was* television.

This got *us* pretty sore. We suspected he was off his rocker, too. Asked him to leave his name and address, but above all to *leave*.

Then he blew his top. Said he was on *the inside* in television. Said he lived in everybody's television set... sees all the television shows... was an authority on modern entertainment... wanted to tell people which ones to look at... said he liked our shows best (*that* old line!) and it was his duty to plug them... etc...

Well, we couldn't get rid of him so we hired him. Figured he couldn't do any harm since the shows he liked are the shows you watch anyway. And there was something about his eyes that appealed to us...

So if he shows up on your set at home, pretend you haven't noticed him and he'll go away. He's sort of dopey, but he can't give you a wrong steer. Because in the major markets where networks compete and their programs can be seen—*and directly compared*, people have liked our shows best over the years.

And this year they look better than ever.

CBS TELEVISION
Channel 2 in New York

CBS Television Network programs on channel 2

ADVENTURE
ACTION IN THE AFTERNOON
ART LINKLETTER'S HOUSE PARTY
ARTHUR GODFREY AND HIS FRIENDS
ARTHUR GODFREY TIME
ARTHUR GODFREY'S TALENT SCOUTS
BEAT THE CLOCK with Bud Collyer
BIG TOWN starring Pat McVey
BLUE RIBBON BOUTS
BOB CROSBY SHOW
CHRONOSCOPE
DANGER
DOUBLE OR NOTHING with Bert Parks
DOUGLAS EDWARDS WITH THE NEWS
ED SULLIVAN'S TOAST OF THE TOWN
FOUR STAR PLAYHOUSE
FRED WARING SHOW
GARRY MOORE SHOW
GENE AUTRY SHOW
GENERAL ELECTRIC THEATER
GEORGE BURNS AND GRACIE ALLEN SHOW
I LOVE LUCY starring Lucille Ball & Desi Arnaz
I'LL BUY THAT with Mike Wallace
I'VE GOT A SECRET with Garry Moore
JACK BENNY SHOW
JACKIE GLEASON SHOW
JACK PAAR SHOW
JUVENILE JURY with Jack Barry
LAMP UNTO MY FEET
LIFE WITH FATHER—Leon Ames & Lurene Tuttle
LOVE OF LIFE
LUX VIDEO THEATRE
MAMA starring Peggy Wood
MAN BEHIND THE BADGE
MAN OF THE WEEK
MEDALLION THEATRE
MEET MILLIE starring Elena Verdugo
MEET MR. McNUTLEY starring Ray Milland
MRS. ALLEN'S SPORTS SPOT
MIRROR THEATRE
MY FAVORITE HUSBAND—Joan Caulfield and Barry Nelson
MY FRIEND IRMA starring Marie Wilson
OMNIBUS with Alistair Cooke
OUR MISS BROOKS starring Eve Arden
PLAY OF THE SPORTS NEWS with Red Barber
PERRY COMO SHOW
PERSON TO PERSON with Edward R. Murrow
PHILIP MORRIS PLAYHOUSE
PLACE THE FACE with Jack Smith
PLAYHOUSE OF STARS
PRIVATE SECRETARY starring Ann Sothern
RED BUTTONS SHOW
RED SKELTON SHOW
ROD BROWN, ROCKET RANGER
SEARCH FOR TOMORROW
SEE IT NOW with Edward R. Murrow
STRIKE IT RICH with Warren Hull
STUDIO ONE
SUNDAY NEWS SPECIAL with Don Hollenbeck
SUSPENSE
THE BIG PAYOFF—Randy Merriman, Bess Myerson
THE BIG TOP with Jack Sterling
THE GUIDING LIGHT
THE JANE FROMAN SHOW
THE LONE RANGER
THE WEB
THIS IS SHOW BUSINESS
TOPPER—Anne Jeffreys, Robert Sterling, Lee G. Carroll
TWO FOR THE MONEY with Herb Shriner
VALIANT LADY
WHAT IN THE WORLD?
WHAT'S MY LINE? with John Daly
WHEEL OF FORTUNE
WINKY DINK AND YOU with Jack Barry
YOU ARE THERE with Walter Cronkite
YOUTH TAKES A STAND

Animated puppet, designed for use in network advertising and on-the-air promotion

THIS IS A HOUSE

Ask a youngster to draw a house, and the chances are he'll top it off with an antenna—almost without thinking about it. The way you used to curl the chimney smoke in your own small-fry pictures.

This may surprise you if you still think of television as a new advertising medium. But a house today is hardly complete without it. Television is part of everyday living in 25 million homes—and a half-million additional sets are installed every month.

For a television antenna is a sign of welcome to people with something to say—and show—in advertising, as in entertainment, sports, news, and public affairs. It's a sign of almost five hours of *daily* welcome on the average screen—which displays products to more people, with more appeal and impact, than any other medium in advertising history.

What assures you the biggest welcome in customers' homes is a good program. And the network with the most popular programs is CBS Television—which consistently wins most of the top ratings where popularity can be compared: *in major markets where networks compete*... It's the network that can take your program—and product—with the greatest economy into American homes. **CBS TELEVISION**

JOEL

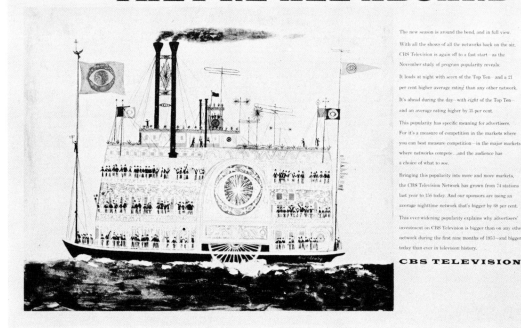

THEY'RE ALL ABOARD

The new season is around the bend, and in full view.

With all the shows of all the networks back on the air, CBS Television is again off to a fast start—as the November study of program popularity reveals.

It leads at night with seven of the Top Ten—and a 21 per cent higher average rating than any other network.

It's ahead during the day—with *eight* of the Top Ten—and an average rating higher by 35 per cent.

This popularity has specific meaning for advertisers. For it's a measure of competition in the markets where you can best measure competition—in the major markets where networks compete...and the audience has a choice of what to see.

Bringing this popularity into more and more markets, the CBS Television Network has grown from 74 stations last year to 156 today. And our sponsors are using an average nighttime network that's bigger by 68 per cent.

This ever-widening popularity explains why advertisers' investment on CBS Television is bigger than on any other network during the first nine months of 1953—and bigger today than ever in television history.

CBS TELEVISION

Three trade ads
tell the network's story
with three different art approaches.

Artists:
Seven-year-old Joel Levy,
Robert Schneeberg
and René Bouché

He can make you happy

Sam Levenson offers you the gift of laughter… he's generous about spreading it around. He's made so many people happy that half of all the sets turned on at Levenson's time are turned on to see Levenson, and that's added up to a 22.5 Trendex rating.

Now he's moved to Tuesday at eight, so that even more people can be happy over his wholesome, effortless humor and inspired story-telling.

One of those people could be a sponsor who knows how family pleasure can carry over into family buying.

That happy sponsor could be you.

◉ CBS TELEVISION

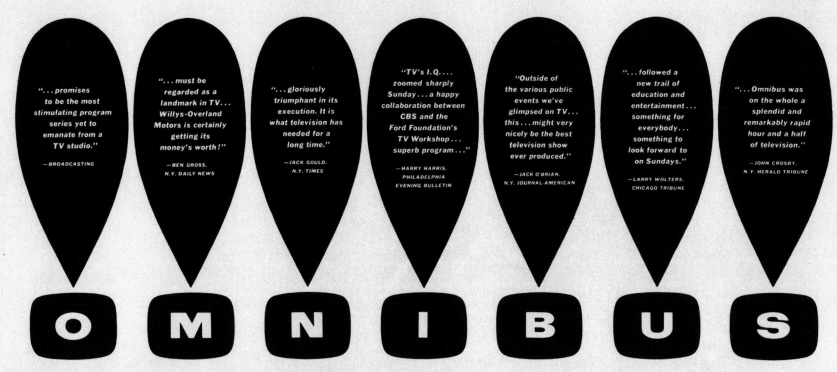

"... promises to be the most stimulating program series yet to emanate from a TV studio."
—BROADCASTING

"... must be regarded as a landmark in TV... Willys-Overland Motors is certainly getting its money's worth!"
—BEN GROSS, N.Y. DAILY NEWS

"... gloriously triumphant in its execution. It is what television has needed for a long time."
—JACK GOULD, N.Y. TIMES

"TV's I.Q.... zoomed sharply Sunday... a happy collaboration between CBS and the Ford Foundation's TV Workshop... superb program..."
—HARRY HARRIS, PHILADELPHIA EVENING BULLETIN

"Outside of the various public events we've glimpsed on TV... this... might very nicely be the best television show ever produced."
—JACK O'BRIAN, N.Y. JOURNAL-AMERICAN

"... followed a new trail of education and entertainment... something for everybody... something to look forward to on Sundays."
—LARRY WOLTERS, CHICAGO TRIBUNE

"... Omnibus was on the whole a splendid and remarkably rapid hour and a half of television."
—JOHN CROSBY, N.Y. HERALD TRIBUNE

O M N I B U S

When the Romans said "Omni[bus]" they meant "for all—for everyb[ody." And that's what we mean, too.

For this is a show that's drawn perhaps the warmest response of anything in television... a b[ig] show, a very big show... whose name can add something to an advertiser. And what it adds is not alone prestige... but along with that, a powerful sal[es] opportunity: opening and closi[ng] credits, a weekly two-minute commercial message, and ever[y] fifth week, a special five-minut[e] program feature—a documentar[y] film based on some aspect of th[e] sponsor's business, produced a[t] no extra cost to him.

Because this show is available to five distinguished sponsors, the cost to each becomes moder[ate] ... the value to each tremendou[s.] It is obviously a program for those advertisers whose astute[ness] matches their importance. Like Willys-Overland Motors, Inc. an[d] The Greyhound Corp., the first Omnibus sponsors.

It is produced by the TV-Radio Workshop of the Ford Foundati[on] and broadcast over the faciliti[es] of the CBS Television Network.

"If you "audition" this Sunday's show (4:30 to 6 pm, New York time)

you'll see Helen Hayes and Burgess Meredith in an original Saroyan play...

another chapter in James Agee's Lincoln story...the Paris Ballet...

a picture of life aboard a tugboat in New York Harbor.

Double-page trade ad
with critics' comments (left)
echoes motif
of program announcement ad (below)

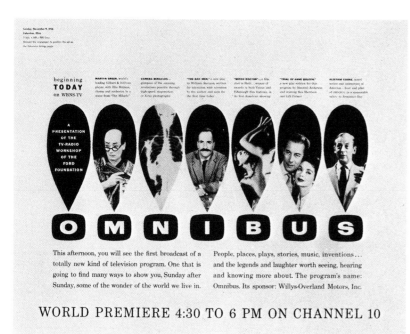

Newspaper ads,
mats, films and slides
illustrate the theme
of the booklet (right)

Studio One presents tonight

The Nativity

The story of the first Christmas as it was first told dramatically in the English language

Tonight television audiences will have the rare opportunity of watching a classic drama about the birth of Jesus based on the text used in medieval England more than six hundred years ago.

Never before broadcast in this country, The Nativity is from an ancient cycle of Mystery Plays performed by the medieval guilds of York and Chester. It will be presented in the language of the original versions, recapturing the grace and pageantry of ancient times.

The famous Robert Shaw Chorale will provide the traditional musical accompaniment to this drama of simple majesty that bridges the ages.

KNXT

Los Angeles

CHANNEL 2

CBS TELEVISION

7 o'clock

Tonight

*Medieval woodcut
sets the mood for the announcement
of a Christmas play.*

*The photographic building blocks (right)
demonstrate the solidity
of the network's program schedule*

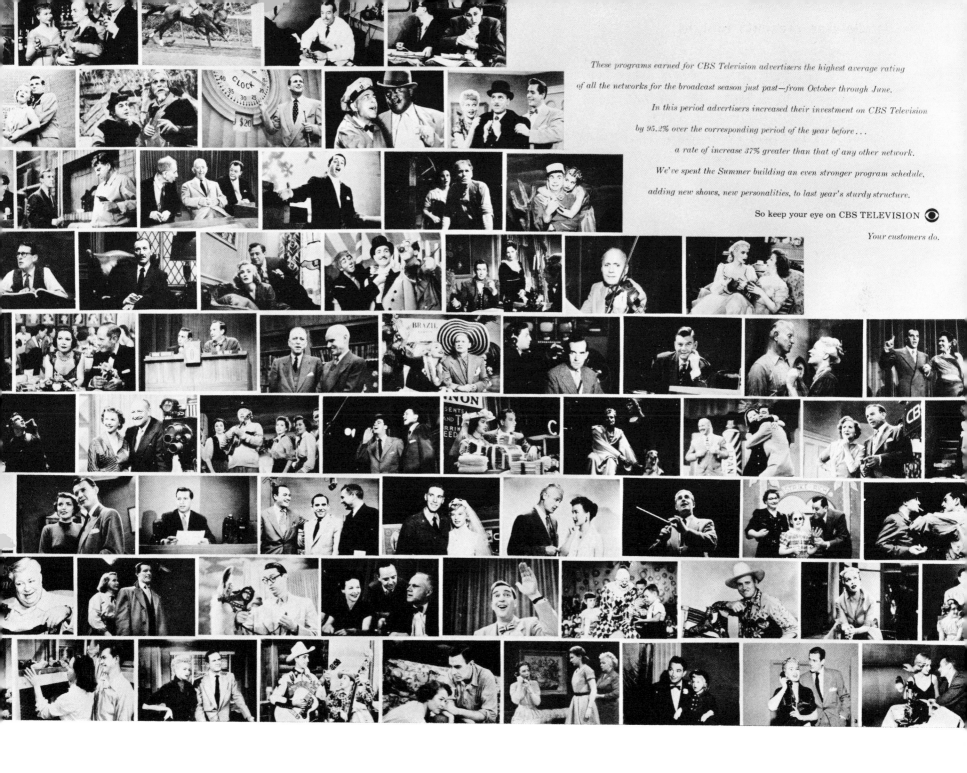

These programs earned for CBS Television advertisers the highest average rating

of all the networks for the broadcast season just past—from October through June.

In this period advertisers increased their investment on CBS Television

by 95.2% over the corresponding period of the year before...

a rate of increase 37% greater than that of any other network.

We've spent the Summer building an even stronger program schedule,

adding new shows, new personalities, to last year's sturdy structure.

So keep your eye on CBS TELEVISION ◉

Your customers do.

A double-page trade ad
illustrates the effectiveness
of sound and vision

One subject—two different techniques:
René Bouché's portrait
and Arnold Newman's photograph
appear on the same day
in different newspapers

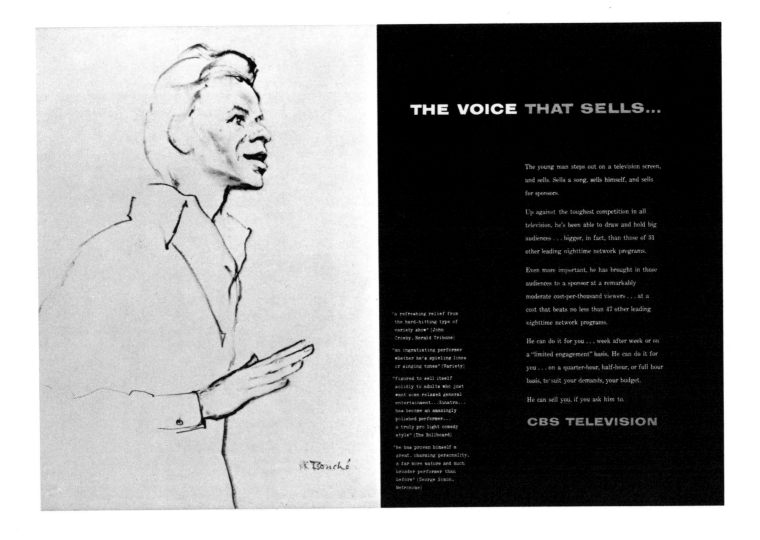

THE VOICE THAT SELLS...

The young man steps out on a television screen,
and sells. Sells a song, sells himself, and sells
for sponsors.

Up against the toughest competition in all
television, he's been able to draw and hold big
audiences . . . bigger, in fact, than those of 31
other leading nighttime network programs.

Even more important, he has brought in those
audiences to a sponsor at a remarkably
moderate cost-per-thousand viewers . . . at a
cost that beats no less than 47 other leading
nighttime network programs.

He can do it for you . . . week after week or on
a "limited engagement" basis. He can do it for
you . . . on a quarter-hour, half-hour, or full hour
basis, to suit your demands, your budget.

He can sell you, if you ask him to.

CBS TELEVISION

"a refreshing relief from
the hard-hitting type of
variety show" (John
Crosby, Herald Tribune)

"an ingratiating performer
whether he's spieling lines
or singing tunes" (Variety)

"figured to sell itself
solidly to adults who just
want some relaxed general
entertainment...Sinatra...
has become an amazingly
polished performer...
a truly pro light comedy
style" (The Billboard)

"he has proven himself a
great, charming personality,
a far more mature and much
broader performer than
before" (George Simon,
Metronome)

RRTBouché.

WARD R. MURROW, broadcasting's most respected reporter, brings a new dimension to television reporting . In his new half-hour program "SEE IT NOW" you will see the exciting potential of television as a news gatherer. ill watch a scrupulously edited report of the week's significant events, some of it on film, some of it happening before your You will meet, face to face, kings and commoners, soldiers and scientists, politicos and plain people who are the masters— victims—of events that affect us all. From your own armchair, you will witness the world.

—*today at 3:30 on the CBS Television Network* **WCBS-TV** *Channel* **2**

EDWARD R. MURROW, broadcasting's most respected reporter, brings a new dimension to television reporting today. In his new half-hour program **"SEE IT NOW"** you will see the exciting potential of television as a news gatherer. You will watch a scrupulously edited report of the week's significant events, some of it on film, some of it happening before your eyes. You will meet, face to face, kings and commoners, soldiers and scientists, politicos and plain people who are the masters— or the victims—of events that affect us all. From your own armchair, you will witness the world.

—*today at 3:30 on the CBS Television Network* **WCBS-TV** *Channel* **2**

The sign
of good
television

When this symbol shines out from a television screen, it identifies, for viewers and advertisers alike, the network where they're most likely to find what they're looking for:

...where 6 of television's 10 most popular shows* are broadcast

...where average ratings are higher than on any other network*

...where television's solid-success package programs come from...shows like Mama, Toast of the Town, Studio One, Suspense, Burns & Allen, Talent Scouts

...where the new hits will *keep* coming from: I Love Lucy, Frank Sinatra, Corliss Archer, See It Now, An Affair of State, Out There, My Friend Irma

...where 59 national advertisers...including 15 of America's 20 biggest...are profitably doing business today.**

"This is the CBS Television Network"

*The network's
on-the-air identification
serves as the theme
of this advertisement.*

*The
continuing importance
of radio
is emphasized in
this 1951
full-page trade ad*

THE NEW YORK TIMES, MONDAY, JUNE 18, 1951

TELEVISION'S BIG BROTHER...

Television's a wonder-child, and no question about it. Precocious as anything, and big for its age. Almost makes you forget that television's got a big brother that can still lick anybody on the block.

Or in the county, or in the country. For network radio is still the only medium that combines *all* advertising essentials: *nation-wide* coverage, thumping impact ...and minimum cost.

That's why the people to whom advertising is most important—the biggest producers of highly competitive products (like drugs, foods and cigarettes)—choose radio above *all* other advertising media, and invest more money there than anywhere. And they keep right on doing it, too, year after year...last year a 2.5% greater network radio investment than they made the year before.

They do this because they know that radio effectively reaches America's *total* market, through 96 million radio sets. And because in spite of all competition, radio continues to grow. (Last year alone there were more *new* radio sets manufactured—over 14½ million—than television's total accumulation of some 12½ million.)

And just as these big advertisers consistently turn to radio, they consistently turn to CBS, investing last year 14.8% more than ever before, 17.3% more than on any other network. The reasons...

They reach more people on CBS...

15 of the 20 *most popular programs*—the bellwethers of radio, that bring more listeners to all programs—are on CBS.

More people listen: the CBS average nighttime audience is 25% larger than that of the second network: daytime, 27% larger.

And they listen *more of the time:* 37% of all nighttime network listening is to CBS (29% to the second-place network).

In rural areas and small towns the CBS habit is even stronger: 41%—to 30% for the second-place network.

Their dollar goes farther on CBS...

The cost-per-thousand of reaching CBS network listeners is $1.18 ...best buy of all the networks. (And to buy that thousand in leading magazines would cost $2.72. And in newspapers, $4.03.)

The big advertisers know better than anybody that you don't send a boy to do a man's work. When there's a big job to be done, you'll want radio...and CBS.

COLUMBIA BROADCASTING SYSTEM

Jerome Snyder

Radio...most versatile entertainer of them all

Nowhere but radio is there such a wide, free choice of entertainment.

Most people the country over find most of the radio programs they like on their CBS Radio station. For the CBS Radio Network has assembled for you and your family the greatest stars, the richest variety of programs, in all entertainment history.

Day in, day out, there's no place like radio...and no radio like CBS Radio.

CBS radio netwo

*Full-color double-pages
promote the radio network
in national magazines.*

*Four paintings show
how each artist attacked
the same subject:
The court jester amuses
the American family*

*Paintings by
Jerome Snyder,
Doris Lee,
Miguel Covarrubias and
Leonard Weisgard*

97

"The radio says   it's going   to rain"

This is probably the commonest remark made in America. Millions of people say it every day. You yourself are always saying it without thinking. You heard it on the radio, so you act on it.

Actually the radio says no such thing. It simply reports what the Weather Man says.

We wish people would think more carefully about radio. But the fact is nobody really thinks about radio. Any more than he thinks about which foot to put in front of the other, or how to blow his nose.

You can quote all the statistics you want about radio's amazing penetration and sales impact to prove what a great medium it is, how much better than any other medium. The statistics are all true and available. But somehow they seem relatively pointless beside the basic fact that people believe what "the radio says."

This is the real secret of radio's power. This is why it is listened to by more people than any other voice in the land. This is why it is such an accepted* voice…such a useful** voice…such a friendly and familiar voice.

Radio doesn't know whether it's going to rain.

Radio is only a voice—anyone's voice. It could even be yours.

Columbia Broadcasting System

*Most accepted: the voice of CBS, reaching 25% more people than that of any other network.

**Most used, too, by U.S. advertisers who invest 15% more on CBS than on any other network.

One of a double-page series featuring the public's dependence on radio

the  _and_  _and you_

Says Variety: "The Egg & I will have little difficulty building a sizable midday audience... most viewers will be presold... should easily nab a sponsor within a few more airings."
Says The Billboard: "the Grade A label predominant... humorous and heartwarming, undeniably rates attention from sponsors. It should get and hold an audience."

All eyes are on this CBS Television Package Program, dressed up with all the topnotch showmanship, cast, and production values that make CBS Television the place both audience and advertisers choose... where 6 of television's 10 most popular programs originate... where average ratings are higher than on any other network. (Trendex, Oct. 1-7)

Here's one show where you concentrate on selling your product, not the show itself. That's already been done. The Egg & I is already beating all the competition in its time period. And because it takes full advantage of one of the biggest box-office titles in modern book and motion-picture history, it's midday television's top sponsor opportunity.

The title of a best seller becomes the illustrated headline of a trade ad

This is CBS...the Columbia Broadcasting System

...where night after night the greatest stars in radio

deliver to advertisers the largest audiences

at the lowest cost of any major advertising medium.

1. The Edgar Bergen—Charlie McCarthy Show
2. Inner Sanctum
3. Beulah (Hattie McDaniel)
4. Lux Radio Theatre (William Keighley)
5. My Friend Irma (Marie Wilson)
6. The Bing Crosby Show
7. You Bet Your Life (Groucho Marx)
8. Mr. Keen, Tracer of Lost Persons (B. Kilpack)
9. Jack Benny (Mary Livingstone, Rochester)
10. Mystery Theatre (Alfred Shirley)
11. The Burns and Allen Show
12. Lowell Thomas
13. Edward R. Murrow with the News
14. Eric Sevareid and the News
15. Meet Corliss Archer (Janet Waldo)
16. Amos 'n' Andy
17. Arthur Godfrey's Talent Scouts
18. Carnation Contented Hour (Ted Dale)
19. Suspense
20. The Bob Hawk Show
21. Dr. Christian (Jean Hersholt)
22. Mr. and Mrs. North (Alice Frost, J. Curtin)
23. The Goldbergs (Gertrude Berg)
24. The Jack Smith-Dinah Shore-Margaret Whiting Show
25. Hallmark Playhouse (James Hilton)
26. Crime Photographer (Staats Cotsworth)
27. My Favorite Husband (Lucille Ball)
28. Skippy Hollywood Theater
29. Leave It To Joan (Joan Davis)
30. Our Miss Brooks (Eve Arden)
31. Dick Haymes' Clu[...] Andrews Sisters,
32. Gangbusters
33. The Vaughn Mon[...]
34. Family Hour of S[...] Jane Wyman, Da[...] Loretta Young, Ir[...]
35. The Gene Autry S[...]
36. Mr. Chameleon ([...]
37. F.B.I. in Peace an[...]
38. The Horace Heidt[...]
39. Sing It Again (Da[...]
40. Life With Luigi (J[...]
41. The Red Skelton[...]

*In a direct mail piece
and a full-color magazine ad
Joe Kaufman shows the performers
behind the entire network schedule*

How to get them into stores

Old store sign on the cover of a mailing piece . . .

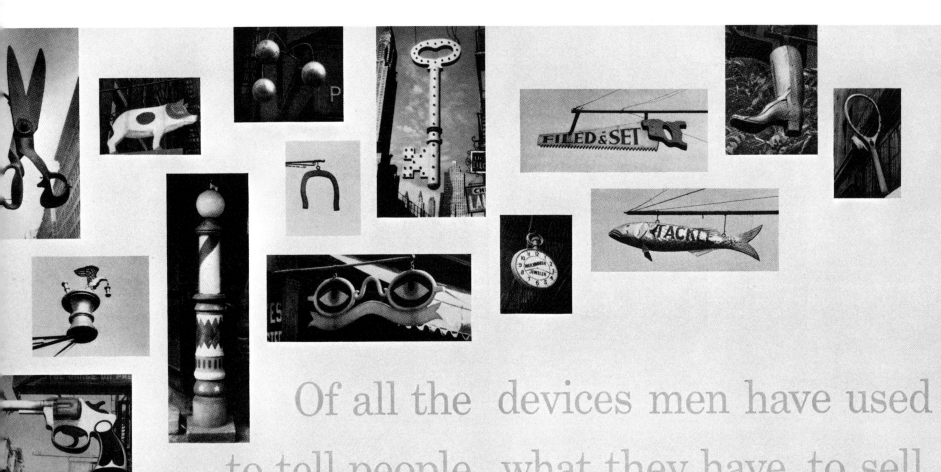

Of all the devices men have used
to tell people what they have to sell,
the most effective is the microphone...

And this one reaches them today
at lower cost than any other advertising medium,
or any other microphone.

Traveling Salesman

. and several similar symbols point up a contemporary selling symbol—the radio mike

An Italian miniature carving . . .

Entertainment has always drawn a crowd. The crowd has always sought it, or waited for it to come to them. Wherever there was a crowd, there were customers. And wherever there were customers, there were people with things to sell. (*A crowd that was in a good mood always bought more.*)

Today the entertainer still gets the crowd, only he gets it faster and bigger. Through radio he reaches crowds of ten and twenty millions in a split second. *And along with him goes the advertiser.*

In radio the largest crowds gather at that point on the dial where the entertainment is the best. That point today is CBS.

For the Columbia Broadcasting System continues to be the most creative network in providing the kind of entertainment which captures the largest audiences.

Only on CBS will you find most of the *sponsored* programs with the largest audiences in radio (11 out of the "top 15").

And only on CBS can advertisers find most of the *available* programs with the largest audiences (7 out of the "top 10").

This is what makes CBS the most effective traveling salesman in radio...reaching more people with better entertainment...making the strongest impressions in all advertising.

A young medium, a young audience.
The snapshot by William Noyes
of his own children,
becomes the illustration
for this 1950 advertisement

The
MAGIC
is built-in

There are two pictures on this page:
the one you are looking at; and the one
they are looking at (which you can't see).

To you the important picture is the people
in front of the television screen. It is a
picture of the special impact achieved only
by this medium, yet which goes far
beyond the novelty of television.

But we are equally concerned with the
picture *on the screen.* For it is the result of
creative programming which alone can
sustain this kind of impact... building into
every program the magic that holds the
largest audiences week in and week out.

It is now clear that CBS is the richest
source of such programming in television
today; that CBS consistently has more
of the most popular programs than any
other network; and that most of these
programs have been created or produced
by the Columbia Broadcasting System.

This picture of television's impact is a
picture any advertiser can create—
but he needs the magic of CBS to hold it.

CBS TELEVISION

. illustrates
that the selling power
of entertainment
has a colorful history

The
sound
of
your
life

Outstanding newsphotos
trace the history of CBS radio
on its 23rd anniversary
in a 136-page book
written by Robert Strunsky

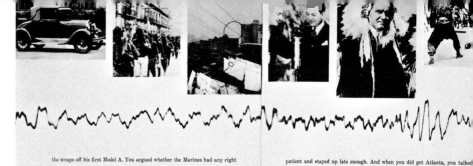

the wraps off his first Model A. You argued whether the Marines had any right to move into Nicaragua. You watched the market soar to new peaks with industrial stocks averaging $214 a share.

The Smiths kept their radio in the living room. It was one of the new Fada Neutrodynes and cost about $95. The loudspeaker was separate and cost extra. Mr. Smith had also rigged up an aerial on the roof. You had to in those days. Otherwise you couldn't hear very well.

The aerial had a lightning switch connected with it. If you were smart you turned it on during storms to keep from blowing up the family. If you were mechanically minded you built your own set, but most of the 7,000,000 radios then in use were sold over the counter.

Like the majority of radio owners, the Smiths listened mostly at night. You could hear better at night and you could get distance. That was the big thing. If you lived in Indiana you might even get Atlanta, Georgia—that is if you were

patient and stayed up late enough. And when you did get Atlanta, you talked about it for days. In 1927 it was hard to get people who had just bought radios to go to bed before 3 a.m.

A Sunday night in September still stands out in the Smiths' memory. It was nearly 9 o'clock and Joe Smith was fiddling with the dial, trying for distance. He brought in the nearby station of WOWO at Fort Wayne and started to tune it out when some words caught his ear. A voice was saying something about the first broadcast of a new radio network called the Columbia Broadcasting System. Then came a list of the call-letters of sixteen stations and the names of the cities in which they were located. The voice was that of Major J. Andrew White, first president of CBS, and he went on to say the new network's first program would be the premiere of a new American opera called "The King's Henchman" by Deems Taylor and Edna St. Vincent Millay. For the next hour the Smiths and hundreds of thousands of other American families from Boston to St. Louis

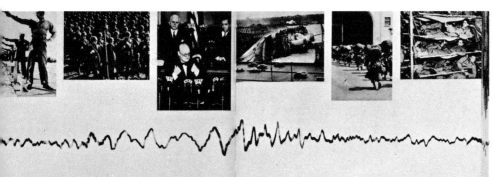

into the record and between the lines.

"Out of the agonies, out of the crisscrossed scars of all the human race, they made a bill of rights for their own people—for a new, a willful and a hopeful nation—made a bill of rights to stand against the enemies within: connivers, fakers, those who lust for power, those who make of their authority an insolence..."

CITIZEN: "Is not our Bill of Rights more cherished now than ever? The blood more zealous to preserve it whole?

"Americans shall answer. For they alone, they know the answer. The people of America: from east, from west, from north, from south."

PRESIDENT ROOSEVELT: "...We will not, under any threat, or in the face of any danger, surrender the guarantees of liberty our forefathers framed for us in our Bill of Rights...

"We are solemnly determined that no power or combination of powers of this earth shall shake our hold upon them."

No other radio drama broadcast before or since reached so large an audience. The listener count was again close to sixty million. Radio again proved itself a formidable channel of strength and inspiration. It repeated this proof the day after Christmas when Winston Churchill addressed the Congress and the people.

CHURCHILL, December 26, 1941: "The wicked men...who have launched their peoples on the path of war and conquest, know that they will be called to terrible account if they cannot beat down by force of arms the people they have assailed...

"Here we are together, defending all that to free men is dear. Twice in a single generation the catastrophe of world war has fallen upon us. Twice in our life-time the long arm of fate has reached out across the oceans to bring the United States into the forefront of the battle...

"Do we not owe it to ourselves, to our children, to tormented mankind, to make sure that these catastrophes do not engulf us for the third time?..."

That winter the Smiths turned to radio as their chief source of news, but the

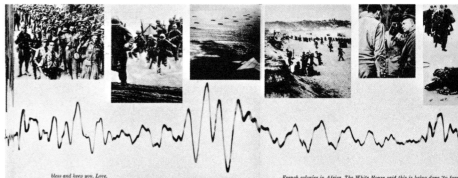

bless and keep you. Love.

"Sign my name and tell my mother how you heard from me."

The tide starts to turn on August 7 when the Marines land on Guadalcanal. It keeps turning with the autumn leaves. At 8:55 p.m. on a November Saturday night, on the network in Washington during a five-minute news period, Eric Sevareid electrifies the country with this sentence:

SEVAREID, November 7, 1942: "...There is tremendous excitement in Axis and neutral capitals about a great Allied convoy, which these capitals say has moved out from Gibraltar into the Mediterranean."

This is all he knows. He turns to other theatres. At 9 his place is taken on the air by the Hit Parade. Mark Warnow and the orchestra swing into Gobs of Love and Joan Edwards takes the chorus. She's cut off in the middle of a high note.

ANNOUNCER: "The White House announced a few minutes ago that powerful American forces are landing on the Mediterranean and Atlantic coast of the

French colonies in Africa. The White House said this is being done 'to forestall an invasion of Africa by Germany and Italy.' British navy and air forces are assisting our troops in the landing. Lieutenant-General Eisenhower is in command of our forces...'"

EDWARD R. MURROW: "Tonight's news will lift British hearts, but there may be no final flourish of trumpets. This may be the turning point of the war..."

Perhaps there were two turning points. In February the Smiths learn by radio of another Valley Forge—the relief of Stalingrad.

NED CALMER, February 2, 1943: "In Russia, the Red Army has written last chapter in this war's story of Verdun. The battle of Stalingrad has ended. That was disclosed by Moscow tonight in a special communiqué, and Joseph Stalin sent his congratulations to the victorious Soviet commanders. The great German siege army of three hundred and thirty thousand men, surrounded since November twenty-third, has been liquidated. The city of the Volga stands unc

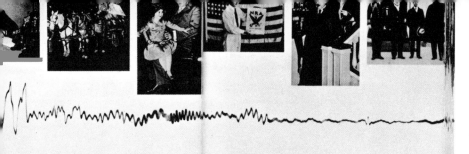

...making his inaugural address at the Capitol:

FRANKLIN D. ROOSEVELT, March 4, 1933: *"Let me assert my firm belief that the only thing we have to fear is fear itself—nameless, unreasoning, unjustified terror which paralyzes needed efforts to convert retreat into advance... We do not distrust the future of essential democracy. The people of the United States have not failed. In their need they have registered a mandate that they want direct, vigorous action. They have asked for discipline and direction under leadership. They have made me the present instrument of their wishes. In the spirit of the gift I take it..."*

This was the very first time the Smiths had happened to hear the voice that was to become perhaps radio's most historic. For Franklin D. Roosevelt was first among the world's public figures to realize fully what an instrument the broadcast human voice could be in explaining and implementing policy. He took his case directly to the people by radio—not alone in public addresses, but in informal "Fireside Chats," and addressed his countrymen as no other head of office had, as "My Friends"—a salutation which was to induce affectionate smiles in many of his listeners, near-apoplexy in others.

But whatever faction they belonged to, it is certain that Franklin D. Roosevelt made very clear to his contemporaries the importance and effectiveness of radio as an instrument of policy. From that day forward, there was never to be a major public issue which was not thoroughly debated and discussed over radio. Leading figures in politics, business, labor, the sciences and professions quickly learned that by carrying their argument or proposal to the people by radio, they could find swifter reaction and response than by any other means. And a lot of public figures began taking voice lessons.

But back there in the chilly March of 1933, the Smiths merely noted there was something comforting about being urged by such a highly-placed person not to fear. And they were glad to be guided by this voice instead of the harsh and stri-

In those 18 days a lot of other people came out with a different answer. This was plainly a new kind of warfare—undeclared, localized, unceasing, and for most Americans radio was the instrument of revelation. Through radio they heard more and understood more of what was happening than any other people in the world. On CBS they heard 417 broadcasts from 18 world news centers by 57 principals. They heard London direct 36 times, Prague 22 times, Paris 15, Berlin 12. They heard events reported and weighed in the now familiar service of international news round-ups, and for the first time they gained a sense of active participation in history in the making.

The fact that Americans found themselves so thoroughly informed was no lucky accident, but the result of the most painstaking care in planning. Since before the Austrian Anschluss, CBS News Director Paul White had been quietly dispatching top news men to all the high-temperature areas of Europe. Elaborate telephone and cable facilities had been arranged for, so that what- ever the emergency, CBS reporters would be there, and able to get the news out.

If you caught on to Hitler's pattern of aggression before Chamberlain did, it could well have been at one of these climactic moments:

CBS ANNOUNCER, September 14: *"Prime Minister Chamberlain will fly to Germany tomorrow to have a personal interview with Adolf Hitler, in a final effort to head off a European war..."*

PHILIP JORDAN (of the London *News Chronicle*) September 17: *"The government is waiting for the visit of French Prime Minister Daladier and Foreign Minister Bonnet...There is a fear that they are coming to discuss...a betrayal without parallel in history."*

WILLIAM SHIRER, September 29 (Prague): *"It took the Big Four just five hours and twenty-five minutes in Munich today to come to an agreement over the partition of Czechoslovakia..."*

Exactly one month later a precocious dramatist of 23 put on the air a

"Here we go again! (Noise) Another plane has come over...right over our port side...tracers are making an arc right over the bow now..."

"...Give it to her, boys!...Another one coming over...a cruiser on...pouring it out...something burning is falling down through the sky and hurtling down ...it may be a hit plane. (Terrific noises in background)...Here he goes...they got one! (Voices cheering) They got one!" (Voice: "Did we?") "Yeah...great splotches of fire came down and are smoldering now just of our port side in the sea...smoke and flame there. (Various sounds and voices in background)... The lights of that burning Nazi plane are just twinkling now in the sea..."

The invasion, the breakthrough, the drive on Paris, a second landing on the Southern coast of France—all go according to plan. Back in the States the same sanguine souls who had looked for invasion in 1943 now say it will all be over by Christmas. Wait and see, they say.

For the Smiths, with a son in Europe, Christmas 1944 is not a merry one. On December 16 the Germans counter-attack south of Aachen. Panzer divisions meet the First Army head on. Leapfrogging paratroopers harass its rear. Next morning Richard Hottelet, at First Army Headquarters, warns it is serious:

"...There's no doubt about it that this is the major German effort. Some of the best units in the German Army are involved in this penetration...

"...There's no hit-and-run character about this. After tanks and infantry made the initial breach the enemy moved his artillery in. He means to consolidate and hold everything he takes and to sustain the offensive..."

Newspapers are now spelling "bulge" with a capital "B." Radio reporters are pronouncing it the same way. Three days before Christmas, in Bastogne, an American brigadier general made of cement and named McAuliffe says "Nuts!" Says it to the German demand for surrender. And means it. He hangs on for another six days and nights, until another American general, for whom "Nuts!" is a term of endearment, puts on one of his memorable

stick their fingers in their ears. A flash lights the sky. In Albuquerque, 120 miles away, a blind girl asks, "What was that?" (It was eight minutes later when she *heard* it.) "That" was the vaporizing of a steel tower, the digging of an excavation three-quarters of a mile wide, the unlocking of a force that binds the universe. That was the first atomic bomb.

On July 26, at Potsdam, Truman and Churchill issue an ultimatum. As the Smiths hear later in the day, it ends with these words:

"We call upon the Government of Japan to proclaim...unconditional surrender ...The alternative for Japan is prompt and utter destruction."

Japan chose the alternative.

On August 6, at 11:15:15 a.m. Harry Kramer interrupts a CBS program:

"...to report a bulletin just received from Washington. President Truman has just announced that an 'atomic bomb' has been used against Japan for the first time, with power equal to 20,000 tons of TNT." On August 9, at 12:31:15 p.m., Joe Weeks interrupts another CBS program: *"The Army has just announced the second use of the atomic bomb, and has announced that good results were obtained. There was no further information..."*

If you were anywhere near a radio in mid-August you know that the Allied nations launched enough V-J Days to end five wars. August 10 wasn't V-J Day though you could cite a picked-up Japanese broadcast to prove it. Nor was it August 11, though the rumors were hot and the owners of store windows anxious. It wasn't August 12, though another premature press association flash said it was. It wasn't the 13th. (A lot of diplomatic finagling was going on. Coded messages shuttled back and forth from Tokyo to Washington, through the neutral capital of Berne. Two sneezes by one Swiss decoding clerk could father half a dozen new rumors.)

At last on August 14, the news breaks at the White House at 7 p.m., on CBS at 7:00:11. By 7:03 Bill Henry is reading the President's statement. It begins:

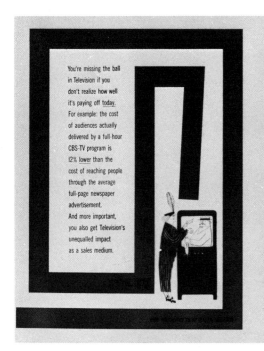

You're missing the ball in Television if you don't realize how well it's paying off today. For example: the cost of audiences actually delivered by a full-hour CBS-TV program is 12% lower than the cost of reaching people through the average full-page newspaper advertisement. And more important, you also get Television's unequalled impact as a sales medium.

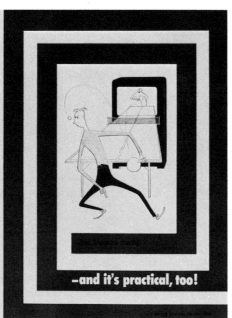

—and it's practical, too!

—and it's practical, too!

With Television only one year old, CBS-TV picked up the ball and ran away with it. Here's what Variety said: "CBS-TV network on the basis of programming, production and showmanship in promoting video as a medium is awarded a Variety Showmanagement plaque for general industry leadership... CBS outstripped its competition."

—and it's practical, too!

—and it's practical, too!

A series of mailing cards modestly states the effectiveness of a new advertising medium.

Leo Lionni's swaggering illustration boasts about radio's reach

It's even
bigger
than
bigger

Each time you look at radio it's bigger.
You turn your head away and before you turn
it back it's bigger than ever.

Radio is bigger than anything—
bigger than magazines, bigger than newspapers,
bigger than both of them put together.

Yet in measuring the bigness of radio,
people still use obsolete yardsticks.
Yardsticks, for example, which compare
the circulation of a *whole* magazine with
the audience of a *single* network program.
(It's like saying my apple-tree is bigger
than your apple, as *Variety* recently put it.)

Or take a yardstick like "cost-per-thousand
listeners." In radio a more realistic gauge
is "**cost-per-million.**" In radio there is
no such thing as only "a thousand" listeners.
(It's like using a ruler to measure the distance
between the stars.)

Sometimes the only way you can tell anything
is bigger than anything is by discovering
that it's smaller. The cost of customers
delivered to advertisers in network radio
is smaller than in any other major medium.

And CBS is both bigger and smaller than
anything in radio—bigger because it delivers
more millions of listeners to advertisers
than any other network; smaller because
it does so at the "lowest **cost-per-million.**"

CBS

—where 99,000,000 people gather every week

The Columbia Broadcasting System

CLOSE-UP

*An 80-page book on television
in its early days.*

*A photographic report
on the dramatic program, "Studio One"
from conception to broadcast.
Writer: Carroll Elliott*

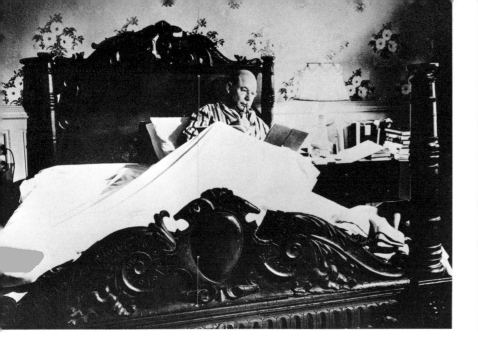

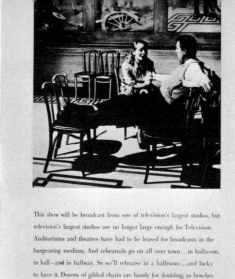

This show will be broadcast from one of television's largest studios, but television's largest studios are no longer large enough for Television. Auditoriums and theatres have had to be leased for broadcasts in the burgeoning medium. And rehearsals go on all over town...in ballroom, in hall—and in hallway. So we'll rehearse in a ballroom...and lucky to have it. Dozens of gilded chairs are handy for doubling as benches and invalids' beds and walls and doorways and office furniture.

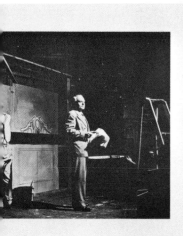

...n't see a stark white or a dead black anywhere...too drastic for ...sitive television tube, which is likely to retaliate by painting an ...d-fog halo around any object so colored. Muted tones are the best ...vision...but you'll see just as much variety and gradation of ...s you would on any stage set. Paint works economic wonders, too... ...ming last week's brick wall into this week's pine-paneled study.

Now at last the efforts of all these people are combined, and facilities rehearsal will show us what we've got. This is a long day and a tough day, of endless experimentation and shifting about of cameras and actors. We must make sure all elements of the show are meshing properly, and we have the smoothest, most effective visual combinations possible.

111

112   *Cover and four pages from a brochure for a documentary program. Artist: Ben Shahn; writer: Robert Strunsky*

who needed care the necessity of obtaining it, and with specific signposts pointed to the ways and means of finding it. These were things that needed to be done. In doing them, "Mind in the Shadow" moved a short distance, at least, into the company of the great social documents of literature—the classic examples of Swift, Dickens, Zola and Hawthorne. In a larger frame, "Mind in the Shadow" did more than this. It reaffirmed Radio's

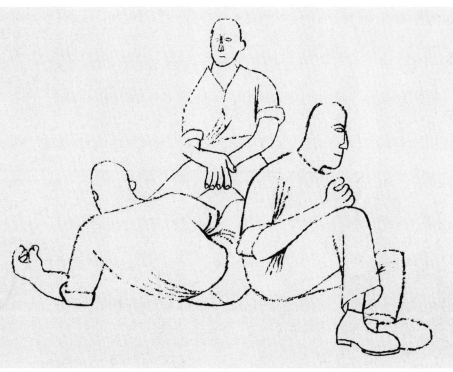

atrists and authorities on mental illness, it won exclamatory praise: "...a grand broadcast. I am terribly proud of it!"—and the request for tran scriptions to be played before various associations and clubs. Irwin Edman, noted author and philosopher, wired CBS: "CONGRATULATIONS ...WONDERFULLY HONEST AND FASCINATING... A REAL CREDIT TO RADIO AND TO YOU."
The press hailed it unanimously: *The New York Times* called it "...an inspiring example."; *The New*

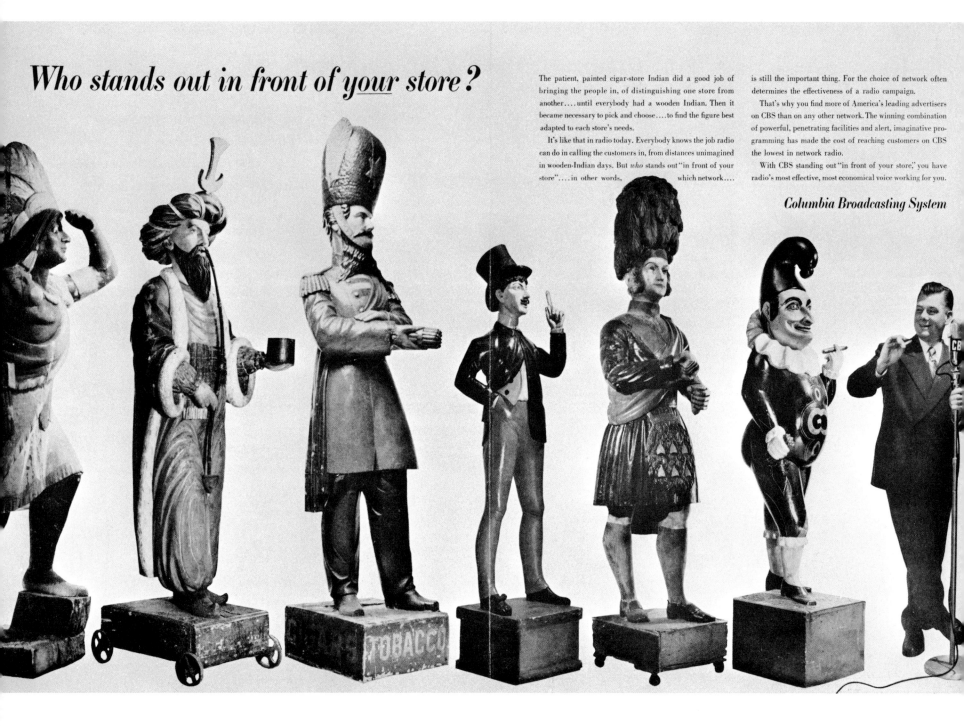

Who stands out in front of your store?

The patient, painted cigar-store Indian did a good job of bringing the people in, of distinguishing one store from another....until everybody had a wooden Indian. Then it became necessary to pick and choose....to find the figure best adapted to each store's needs.

It's like that in radio today. Everybody knows the job radio can do in calling the customers in, from distances unimagined in wooden-Indian days. But *who* stands out "in front of your store"....in other words, which network....

is still the important thing. For the choice of network often determines the effectiveness of a radio campaign.

That's why you find more of America's leading advertisers on CBS than on any other network. The winning combination of powerful, penetrating facilities and alert, imaginative programming has made the cost of reaching customers on CBS the lowest in network radio.

With CBS standing out "in front of your store," you have radio's most effective, most economical voice working for you.

Columbia Broadcasting System

Cigar store figures link radio to a vanished American tradition. Photo: Ben Rose

it is now tomorrow...

Look closely at your new horizon.

These are not the shapes of things to come, but of things already here.

For in Autumn 1949, television in its **full** proportions is clearly visible...creating new patterns in the basic habits of Americans. It is changing the way they work and play; the way they think and talk, and buy and sell.

In this pattern, the habit of tuning to CBS Television is firmly fixed —held fast by powerful programming like The Goldbergs...Studio One... Arthur Godfrey...Ed Wynn...Mama ...Suspense...Inside U.S.A....

And as they tune to CBS be sure they see *your* product among those of America's great advertisers— making sharp, lasting impressions today and tomorrow.

CBS *television*

first in audiences

Paul Strand records the emerging new skyline

It takes
the right kind
of bait...

And in Boston, it's WEEI!

Here's proof: WEEI's E. B. Rideout—for 23 years "the weatherman" to New England listeners —talked about Rusco storm windows for E. A. Parlee Company, at 6:45 three mornings a week. His first nine broadcasts netted 1,500 new orders. A haul of exactly $37,500 in sales!

No wonder more Boston advertisers invest more money—and make more sales— on WEEI than on any other station!

WEEI

"COLUMBIA'S FRIENDLY VOICE IN BOSTON"

Represented by Radio Sales . . . Radio Stations Representative, CBS

mig

ctive!

In Boston, 8 out of the 10 top-rated
local programs are on WEEI.*
In fact, all week long "Columbia's
friendly voice in Boston" delivers
the biggest rating more often than all
other Boston stations combined!
Want to make a big "flutter" in Boston
without getting burned in the process?
Ask us or Radio Sales to tell you
more about one of these mighty
attractive programs on ... **WEEI**

*Pulse of Boston, Nov.-Dec. 1949

Bugs in your Boston   Budget?

WEEI in Boston can get rid of them. Fast!

Like this: Six years ago, Eldred & Barbo—
furniture manufacturers— opened a store
14 miles from Boston. They bought participations
on WEEI's "Priscilla Fortescue." Today, with a
three-acre showroom, they call themselves
"the business Priscilla built," and say, "she
brings us more customers than four
other Boston stations combined!"

No wonder more Boston advertisers invest more
money—and make more sales—on WEEI
than on any other   station.

...*it's so easy to listen*

And since 1941 — when this photograph was made — it has
become even easier to listen to CBS.

That's one reason why one network, CBS, with its 99,000,000
different listeners each week, reaches more people than
read all the magazines published in the United States.

For CBS today has achieved the best "balance" of facilities
in all Radio, with more high-powered, and fewer low-powered
stations, than any other network. And since 1941 almost
every CBS station — 150 out of 162 — has made specific
major technological improvements.

In the past year alone, CBS stations have added 230,000 watts
of extra power; far more power than any other network increase —
almost as much added power as all the other networks combined.

No wonder that CBS delivers its large audience to advertisers
at a lower cost than any other network. And that latest reports
show that the largest individual audiences in all radio are
the CBS audiences of the LUX RADIO THEATRE in the evening,
the ARTHUR GODFREY show in the daytime.
And that more of the hundred largest users of Radio are
on CBS than on any other network.

Columbia Broadcasting System
— where 99,000,000 people gather every week

Radio versus magazines:
A media comparison advertisement,
supported by
a documentary photograph

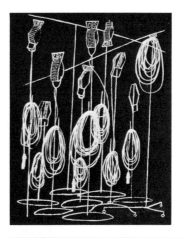

The empty studio...

The drawings by Ben Shahn
set the stage
for the drama of a medium
—radio,
in a four-page folder

Ben Shahn

121

The Son of Man

A PASSION PLAY FOR RADIO

*An important radio documentary
is introduced
in this mailing piece,
with drawings by Ben Shahn*

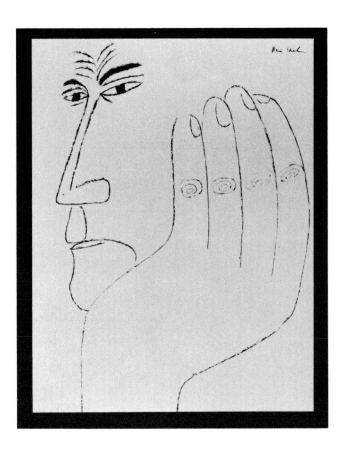

The Columbia Broadcasting System

and its affiliated stations present

"fear begins at forty"

A production of the CBS Documentary Unit. Tuesday, October 28, 9:30-10:30 p.m. EST

THE CBS Documentary Unit, for this major production of the 1947 Fall season, turns from its study of youth (THE EAGLE'S BROOD) and medicine (A LONG LIFE AND A MERRY ONE) to consideration of the problem of those who are "too old" …"too old" to be employed, "too old" to maintain themselves with dignity, "too old" to make the economic and cultural contributions of which they are still capable.

And this is a logical turning of the spotlight, for the medical and scientific accomplishments which give Americans greater life-expectancy, have also helped to create another problem: the problem of old age for more and more people.

It is a real and growing problem: in 1900, only 17% of the U.S. population were 45 or over; in 1940, the total had grown to 26.5%; by 1980, it is estimated, 40% of the total U. S. population will be 40 or over.

And today, between 13 and 14 million people in the U.S. are over 60.

What are the problems of the man (or woman) standing on the threshold of 40, and looking down the years ahead to 60? What are the problems of this steadily increasing group of the "too old"? How are they being met in our country today?

What of the "homes" designed to care for them? What of job security? What of Social Security? What of the vast waste of human happiness? What of the economic waste? What do we spend yearly on geriatrics, that subdivision of medicine concerned with old age and its diseases? In short, what do we do about one of America's most pressing problems?

FEAR BEGINS AT FORTY is the thoughtful, dramatic posing of these questions, met by the CBS Documentary Unit researchers and staff writers as they set about assembling the material that has gone into the program.

FEAR BEGINS AT FORTY presents, through the true story of one American family, the composite experiences, the hundreds of actuality bits and pieces encountered by CBS researchers in their talks with sociologists; their visits to "homes for the aged"; their interviews with men turned from work because of age; their visits to employment bureaus; their studies of rows and rows of faceless figures, sightless statistics.

FEAR BEGINS AT FORTY is an engrossing dramatic presentation of a problem confronting many Americans today, to confront many more tomorrow. Using the techniques which distinguish the CBS Documentary Unit, FEAR BEGINS AT FORTY will, we believe, bring home to Americans the necessity for thoughtful action on a problem that concerns us all.

FEAR BEGINS AT FORTY poses the specific problem of the "too old". It is the problem of the young as well. They must solve this problem which must sooner or later become theirs.

The Philharmonic radio concerts
are the subject of a series of drawings
in a brochure
on audience reactions.
Artist: Jean Pages
Writer: Robert Strunsky

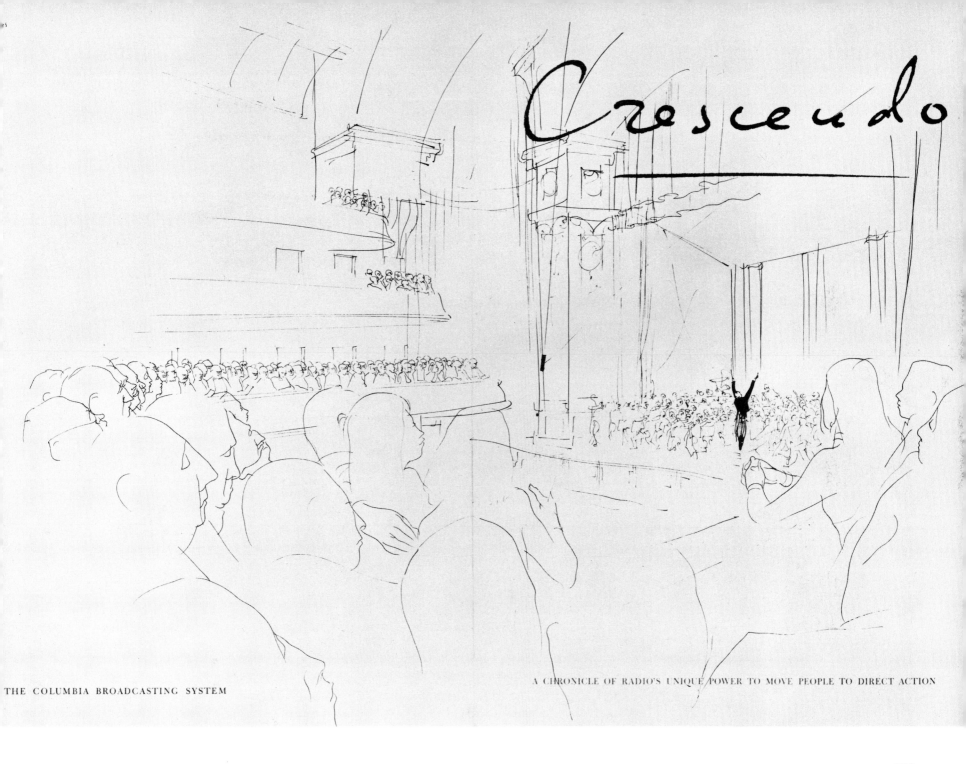

Crescendo

THE COLUMBIA BROADCASTING SYSTEM

A CHRONICLE OF RADIO'S UNIQUE POWER TO MOVE PEOPLE TO DIRECT ACTION

125

Bill *by Ben Shahn*

To discuss the work and the character of Bill Golden is, for me, to discuss graphic design itself, what it should be, what it can be in the most skilled and sophisticated hands. My association with Bill was my first contact with the world of graphic design. I sometimes wonder whether, if that contact had been with a less obstreperous antagonist, it might not have been my last.

That first contact might better be called the first round. I had been invited to work in the Office of War Information with, or under—I'm not sure which—a Bill Golden, whose name had been mentioned with the profoundest respect. I hadn't yet learned to whisper the great names in design. Perhaps I still haven't, but I have come to recognize that this creative field has been developed to great heights within our present era, and that one of the people most responsible for such an achievement has been Bill Golden.

Our first round concerned a war poster. We sat together through a session or two and discussed what a war poster ought to be. It must be neither tricky nor smart. Agreed. The objective is too serious for smartness. It has to have dignity, grimness, urgency. Agreed. It has to be unblinkingly serious; agreed. We then began to suggest, discard, work toward specific image ideas. We agreed upon such an image idea and I undertook it at home over a weekend. I felt its urgency and did not want to undertake it in the unresolved atmosphere of the OWI studio.

Once I had begun to put our poster idea into image form, I became acutely aware of fallacies in it that would never have emerged in a simple conversation. I played around a little with the idea, then came up with a new one, totally different, that was visual and not verbal. It was ultimately known as the *French Workers* poster.

Bill's reaction to what I had created was apoplectic. It wasn't what we had talked about or what we had agreed upon. If (I said to myself) he expected me to labor and belabor an idea that was neither visual nor valid, he was working with the wrong artist.

I think that both Bill and I solidified our graphic futures more through that impasse than through any subsequent single experience. What I learned was a hardened determination to put the integrity of an image first and above all other considerations; one must be prepared to retire from any job whatever and to let someone else make either a mess or a success of it, rather than abandon the clear vision that he may have. I took this position.

I believe that what Bill discovered then—although he did not yield on the matter of the poster—was that you get your visual material in hand and look at it. Then you begin to design.

That we remained, or rather, became friends may seem amazing. Perhaps neither of us had ever met with quite so much cussedness before. But then my own respect for him soared when I first saw the photographic war posters that he had designed. These were unblinkingly stark photographs, each surrounded by a thick black line. Their impact was tremendous and entirely uncluttered by unessential messages. I began to develop a respect and affection for this fellow that nothing would ever weaken, and there is no doubt that Bill returned my liking in fullest measure.

He went into the army; I remained with the OWI. I often used his New York apartment; he often visited me and my family. We found ourselves in deepest agreement politically, personally, and in art and food. We talked about everything under the sun except the *French Workers* poster which, during this time, had been produced and was being sought considerably by collectors. I never found out what Bill thought of it.

When Bill was out of the army and had returned to CBS, he called and asked whether I would do a folder with him on a subject that he thought I would like. That was on the growing problem of delinquency in the United States, a program to be called *The Eagle's Brood*. I twitted Bill a little, telling him that I had noted my name on the desk of a Philadelphia art director as an artist "not to be directed."

My innuendoes were unnecessary. Bill didn't even give me a size. I was indeed deeply moved by the material in hand, and especially by the treatment given it in the CBS program. I made a drawing that, to me, very well expressed both the compassion and the anger that the situation aroused, and I took it to Bill.

From that time on we worked together in complete understanding and remarkable co-ordination. Bill's use of my drawing gave it a new importance — there was no question about that and I think I had the good grace to tell him so. Bill had also discovered a printer—Eddie Katz—no mean asset to any designer's talent—and together they presented me with a reproduction that I found pretty breath-taking. After that, we did many kinds of graphic jobs together, from full-page newspaper advertisements to the book of *Hamlet*, that quintessence of elegance, and one of the last pieces of work that we did

together. Every job was a delight, the results always a pleasure.

I hardly need to go into the years of Bill's development of the visual world with which he surrounded the name of CBS. But I might point out that he clothed the name with a distinction, an aura which other stations and a good many advertisers sought to emulate. They could, and usually did, imitate the latest piece that Bill had created, but they could never anticipate the next. The qualities Bill brought to graphic presentation could not be matched.

I would say that the first of these qualities was simply scope. Bill had read enormously; his thinking was clear and bold. The world of advertising and publicity exercised no tyranny over him. He didn't give a damn about what was considered the latest mode in his profession—indeed that was something to be avoided. His interest was to create something new. That he did, and he created it out of his vast understanding and concern with the whole world. Bill was interested in art, not

just the art of his own sphere of operations, but in all art. He was interested in politics, in publications both little and big, and above all in people. Oddly enough, he was not social; his cocktail tolerance was practically nil. His interest in people was, rather, a vast compassion for the hurt, the timid and the beaten-down. Out of this abiding belief and feeling of his, came, it seems to me, the basic energy, the motive-power of everything that he did.

Unlike so many other publicity people, he was incapable of cynicism toward the public. The public, insofar as it can be looked upon as the simple, ordinary fellow, was his God. He could neither outrage nor abuse it—in that profession in which outrage and abuse of public sensibilities are the order of the day! But I do believe that one of the basic reasons why his work could not be easily imitated was just because his motivations were so deep and so genuine. His life-work was to bring something of highest quality into the public ken, to elevate public standards,

never to be guilty of depressing them.

One of the saddest maladies of the public picture world is that frenzied clamoring to capture the style of this or that innovator. Of course it is quite possible to ape the surface look of a piece of work. If I use ragged black lines, so can the next fellow (and don't they, though!). If Bill Golden uses a black line around a poster, so can someone else. But style is the product of a temperament; it is that arrangement of elements which fulfills the inner need of meaning. Such meanings are one with the personal values of an individual: they are the meanings of his convictions, his experience, his education, his objectives and his attitude toward people. A black line around a gasoline poster may be eye-catching, but will have no meaning (at least no intentional one). But a black line around a poster telling of atrocities against people is a line of anger. That is what style is and why it cannot be imitated. That is why Bill was a great designer and why his imitators are only imitators.

Patron-art director   *by Feliks Topolski*

At the end of the war Cipe Pineles (in uniform) brought to my blitz-battered studio in London a most handsome G.I. This grand specimen of athletic, blond, fine-featured American manhood (greeted therefore with some reserve) proved within minutes that, unbelievably, his handsomeness embraced his spirit. Within an hour we were settled into a lifetime friendship.

This friendship was true. That is, we met seldom, divided by distances and duties, but it was there (unaided by correspondence), always ready.

An artist is and always was dependent on his patron, whether a king, a pope, an art dealer, a committee—or an art director. (With the exception of artists of the end of the XIXth and the beginning of this century—fanatics sustained by revolutionary and group spirit. Since then artistic revolutions have become institutionalized.) And I do not mean just materially. Even the mighty genius, Michelangelo, however recognized and respected, wrestled with his patrons continuously and was often thwarted for opportunities to match his powers and for money to match his needs. How unfulfilled he would have been without the Sistine Chapel!

And so, throughout art's history, the artist gave all of his potential, or better still, surpassed himself when given trust and opportunity; or, conversely his talents withered or became corrupted when held down by the indifference or vanity of his patron.

Today, the vanity and vulgarity—not exclusively of advertising patrons, but also of museum directors and art dealers — play ruthless power games with artistic reputations—in order to manipulate, or keep up with, the current market for whatever is fashionable.

The power of today's art officials, art salesmen and art critics (the middlemen of "high art") functions without any brakes and constitutes a dangerous and erratic tyranny.

An art director is a patron of the traditional order. His power is tempered by responsibility not unlike that of the patrons of old—the churches and rulers who propagated and stabilized through the artists their heavenly or earthly kingdoms. However, our time is dominated by the sales fallacy which demands not instruction but provision of the imaginary "what the public wants." Thus the art director, as an art patron, can easily stray.

Bill Golden, after five, eleven, twelve years (these were the years we met and worked together), unchanged physically (strong, calm and young), proved himself reassuringly a model patron.

To list his qualities as an art director is to set a seemingly impossible ideal. Yet he was all this:

—a supreme judge: he disentangled unerringly the exploring masters from the cultivators—followers of the widest range of "styles." He was never a slave to current prejudices.

—modest: he had none of the oft met arrogance of "knowing-better" and bending the artist to the art director's idea—but, having set his protegé on a widely conceived project, he would follow along and develop his own concept on the basis of the artist's work.

—reliable: with unwavering judgment and instinct and unquestioned authority, he generated a relaxed and fertile mood for creative cooperation.

— straightforward, considerate and patient: men of money and power often lack assurance and so they employ amongst many others, the intimidation gimmicks: difficulty of approach, aloof posturing and exclusiveness toward the artist on whom their glory depends. Bill was a friend, at ease with his artists, eager to keep them *au courant* with the work in progress with proofs and reports, helpful in work and life, hospitable, generous in sharing his friends and his "contacts."

—supreme craftsman: his gifts were thanks to his instinct and wisdom, nourished on the best work provided by the best artists.

The list is far from complete in more senses than one. This powerful, calm man contained still unreleased energies in plenty. He seemed so undiminished by the passage of time.

A tribute to William Golden   *by John Cowden*

*(On May 13, 1960 the National Society
of Art Directors posthumously
presented its annual award of Art Director
of the Year to the late William Golden
in recognition of his influence and
achievements over many years in the
field of advertising design.
The Award was presented to his widow,
Mrs. Cipe Pineles Golden, at a dinner
given by the Philadelphia Art Directors
Club at the Poor Richard Club
in Philadelphia.
In connection with the presentation of
the Award, John Cowden, Vice President
of the CBS Television Network,
recalled his long friendship
and association with Mr. Golden
throughout his career with the Columbia
Broadcasting System and paid tribute
to his outstanding contributions to
the company.)*

---

*On the following twenty pages
is a condensed pictorial record
of a typical year's (1957) output
by William Golden
and his design associates*

It would be hard to conceive of any obstacle that could keep me from taking part in an occasion that does honor to Bill Golden. At the same time I was extremely hesitant to speak this evening since, unlike Bill and most of you here tonight, I know little about design and graphic arts. What finally gave me courage was the thought that I could make capital out of my shortcoming.

For one thing it enables me to talk mainly about Bill himself — to speak about him in relation to his work, to the people he worked with, and to the company whose interests were always uppermost in his mind. As for the product of that mind: I am going to let his work speak for itself. Not being a designer perhaps has another advantage. It may make it easier for me to look behind and beyond his ads and mailing pieces, past his awards and citations and see the extraordinary qualities that made up this remarkable man.

When I met him for the first time in 1938, he was then one of a group of layout artists in the bull pen of the CBS

Radio Network's Advertising Department, and I was an apprentice in the Copy Department—in other words, his natural enemy. I had not been there for more than a few weeks before I discovered that one of Bill's closest friends and greatest admirers in the company was a young man who had been recently appointed head of the Research Department. His name was Frank Stanton. Although they differed markedly in personality and background—Golden was a New York boy, Stanton grew up in a small Middle Western town — and although one worked with a slide rule, the other with a T square—they shared a common philosophy about their work and in particular about advertising.

They were both perfectionists. They were both deeply committed to the principle of form. They were both animated by the conviction that the only possible way for advertising to command attention and be remembered was to present each message so distinctively that it would stand out in bold relief from all others. They recognized that within the field of media advertising generally, and broadcasting specifically, there was often little difference between the claims and counterclaims of one company and another. And since CBS advertising was primarily aimed at advertisers and agencies, they realized that if special attention and emphasis were given to *form* it would meet with particular response on the part of the professional and sophisticated groups to which the advertising was directed.

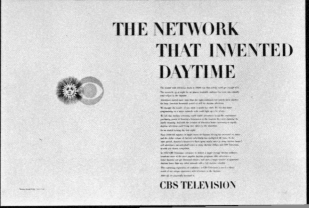

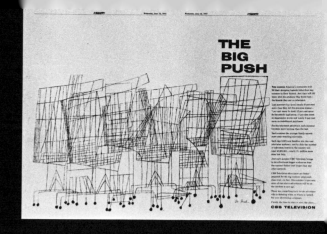

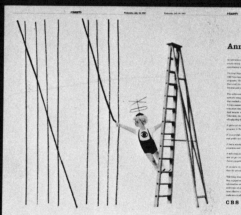

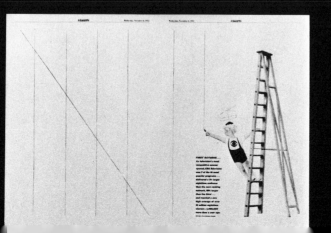

Moreover, they were fortunate in enjoying the support of a management that was equally committed—in the person of the late Paul Kesten—to the value and power of advertising—a commitment that was matched by a professional appreciation and interest in good promotion. Thus, the Advertising Department at CBS was never regarded solely as a service function—that is to say, as exclusively the tool of the sales force or the servant of the Program Department. It was considered to have its own separate identity and function —namely to be the voice of management and to enhance and sustain the CBS image. This thesis was tested and proved in the early days when the CBS Radio Network had neither the stars nor the facilities nor the advertising support enjoyed by its major competitors. Yet CBS advertising created the *impression* that it was equally strong, and in so doing helped to transform this impression into a reality.

The friendship and sense of mutual purpose that characterized the relationship between Bill Golden and Frank Stanton grew even stronger as it became a day-to-day professional association with Stanton's appointment as Advertising Director, and continued to flourish throughout the years, as Stanton took over the reins as President of the Columbia Broadcasting System.

The two men kept in constant touch. They talked a language all their own. Scarcely an ad was produced by Bill

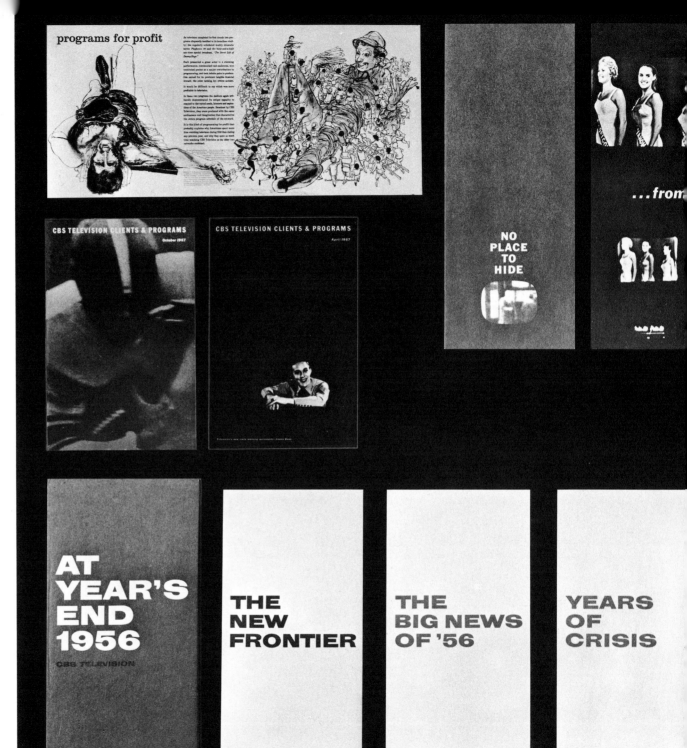

The
Multiple Target
of Industrial
Advertising

Merle S. Jones

Rate Card = 13

CBS
TELEVISION
NETWORK

effective March 10, 1957

1958

A CBS TELEVISION NETWORK PROGRAM

ACT
OF
MAGIC

At the stroke of 8, on Sunday night March 31, nearly every home in the nation witnessed an act of electronic magic that only television can perform.

It presented this 300-year-old tale, infused with life and song especially for television by two master magicians of the theatre, and gave it a new kind of opening night.

It was one that television itself had never seen.

It was scheduled on 245 stations for broadcast over practically the entire continent of North America —the largest number of television stations ever assembled by a network for a single program.

It was watched by an audience of more than 100,000,000—the largest number ever to view an entertainment program—enough, as someone pointed out, to fill a Broadway theatre 7 days a week for 165 years.

By capturing and enthralling virtually an entire population simultaneously, it demonstrated again the medium's unique power not only to satisfy the public's increasing interest in television but also the advertiser's need for vast audiences.

It offered further evidence that even a fabulous program can attract still more spectacular audiences when it is broadcast over a network with the most popular program schedule in television.

CBS TELEVISION

A
TELEVISION
NOTEBOOK

with drawings by Carl Erickson

CBS TELEVISION
1958

PROGRAM PROMOTION MATERIAL FOR LOCAL STATIONS

that did not get an immediate reaction from Stanton. Most of the time it was just a line, such as "Great job! Wish I could say the same for the show"—or a childlike sketch of a face wearing a wide grin. On those rare occasions when an ad didn't quite come off, or when the publication botched up the reproduction, the sketch came downstairs showing the same face, this time with the grin turned down and a couple of tears streaming from the eyes.

But even such criticism was heartening, too. It showed that someone cared —and cared deeply—about everything the department was doing.

However, it would be a grave error to infer that Bill's success depended on the happy accident of working at a company with such a philosophy toward advertising. The blunt fact is that the CBS advertising philosophy is to a very large extent his own creation. For it was he more than anyone else who, by the sheer force of personality, pride in profession, and faith in his own ability, hammered out an advertising philosophy for CBS and then forced everyone to stick to it whenever the pressure mounted to compromise with principle.

Nothing upset him more than someone who alibied his samples on the ground that his particular client would not let him do good work. Bill maintained—and proved it at CBS—that there are no good or bad clients, there are only good or bad advertising men. And he accepted the fact that part of the responsibility of being an advertis-

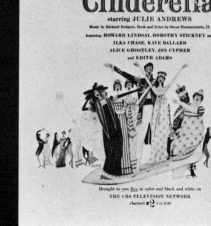

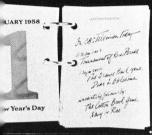

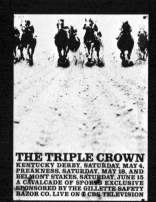

ing man and a designer was to have the courage of one's convictions . . . a bulldog tenacity . . . a willingness to do daily battle for the things one believed in . . . and the recognition that constant vigilance is the price of freedom.

Many years ago, when he was offered the title of Vice President in charge of Advertising and Sales Promotion, he said no thanks. His reasons were significant—and characteristic. He said the stripes would be bars . . . that they would force him to become a "company man" . . . to take the so-called "broad view" at the expense of principle.

Bill preferred to keep his independence and to preserve his inalienable right to shout—when the occasion demanded—that the emperor wasn't wearing any clothes. In any case, he said he didn't want to go to meetings, or be snowed under by administrative duties. I mention this because it reveals how Bill was willing to sacrifice anything—including his own advancement—if he felt it stood in the way of better design and advertising.

The story, incidentally, has an ironic but delightful ending. In scorning the conventional status symbols, Bill won far more. By turning down a vice presidency, he eventually gained a respect and status that outranked any vice president in the company.

This integrity and pride in craft were also apparent in his willingness to lay his job on the line if anyone tried to invade his special area of responsibility. I remember a layout for a rate

126

PLAYHOUSE 90

3:30 PM TODAY CHANNEL 2
KHRUSHCHEV
FACE THE NATION
ON CBS TELEVISION

PLAYHOUSE 90
THE DEATH OF MANOLETE
JACK PALANCE
SUZY PARKER
9:30 TONIGHT
ON CHANNEL 2

STUDIO ONE
THE NIGHT AMERICA TREMBLED
EDWARD R. MURROW
TONIGHT AT 10 ON CHANNEL 2

I'VE GOT A SECRET
TONIGHT AT 9:30 ON CHANNEL 2

LASSIE
TONIGHT AT 7 ON CHANNEL 2

PERSON TO PERSON
BACK TONIGHT AT 10:30 CHANNEL 2

BEAT THE CLOCK
MONDAY THROUGH FRIDAY AT 2 PM CHANNEL 2

THE JIMMY DEAN SHOW

8 PREMIERE TODAY
AT NOON ON CHANNEL 2
HOTEL COSMOPOLITAN

COLTS VS. REDSKINS
TODAY AT 2:00 PM ON CHANNEL 2

PREMIERE TONIGHT @ 9:30
RICHARD BOONE...HAVE GUN-WILL TRAVEL
GUNSMOKE-TONIGHT AT 10
CHANNEL 2, CBS TELEVISION

TONIGHT
THE PHIL SILVERS SHOW-AT 8
PREMIERE
THE EVE ARDEN SHOW-8:30
CHANNEL 2, CBS TELEVISION

REX HARRISON STARS IN
CRESCENDO
PRODUCED BY
PAUL GREGORY
JULIE ANDREWS
LOUIS ARMSTRONG
EDDY ARNOLD
DIAHANN CARROLL
CAROL CHANNING
BENNY GOODMAN
STANLEY HOLLOWAY
MAHALIA JACKSON
SONNY JAMES
STUBBY KAYE
PEGGY LEE
LIZZIE MILES
TURK MURPHY
DINAH WASHINGTON
DU PONT SHOW OF THE MONTH
CHANNEL 2 TONIGHT
9 TO 10:30 PM

DOUGLAS EDWARDS WITH THE NEWS
TONIGHT AT 7:15

GENERAL ELECTRIC THEATER
TONIGHT AT 9

THE ADVENTURES OF ROBIN HOOD
TONIGHT AT 7:30

ALFRED HITCHCOCK PRESENTS-9:30
CBS TELEVISION, CHANNEL 2

PREMIERE TONIGHT AT 7:30 ON CHANNEL 2
Bachelor Father

THE VERDICT IS YOURS

MISS AMERICA PAGEANT
TONIGHT AT 10:30 ON CHANNEL 2

CBS Television Premiere
tonight at 8:00 on channel 2
THE BIG RECORD
PATTI PAGE

RED SKELTON
CBS TELEVISION 9:30 PM, CHANNEL 2

THE MILLIONAIRE
TONIGHT AT 9 ON CHANNEL 2

7:30 TONIGHT
PERRY MASON
STARRING RAYMOND BURR
AND AT 8:30 STAY TUNED TO CHANNEL 2
Dick and the Duchess

I LOVE LUCY
Tonight at 7:30
And at 8 stay tuned for
THE BIG RECORD
PATTI PAGE
CHANNEL 2

PLAYHOUSE 90
Topaze
ERNIE KOVACS
CARL REINER
RICHARD HAYDN
SHEREE NORTH
TONIGHT 9:30
CHANNEL 2

TONIGHT AT 10
THE U.S. STEEL HOUR
presents Edward Mulhare and Dorothy Collins in WHO'S EARNEST?
LIVE ON CHANNEL 2

10 TONIGHT ON CHANNEL 2
STUDIO ONE
The Deaf Heart
starring Piper Laurie

THE BIG RECORD
PATTI PAGE

OUR MISS BROOKS
CBS Television 2 pm, channel 2

ARTHUR GODFREY TIME
live on CBS Television

THE BOB CROSBY SHOW
live on CBS Television 3:30 pm, channel 2

"Knight In Shining Armor"
THE BIG PAYOFF
live on CBS Television 3 pm, channel 2

SEARCH FOR TOMORROW
on CBS Television 12:30 pm

THE JIMMY DEAN SHOW
live on CBS Television 7 am, channel 2

RICHARD MOTTELET WITH THE NEWS
live on CBS Television channel 2

CAPTAIN KANGAROO
8 am, channel 2

THE EDGE OF NIGHT
4:30 pm, channel 2

THE LINEUP
BACK TONIGHT AT 10 ON CHANNEL 2

HARBOURMASTER
PREMIERE TONIGHT AT 8 ON CHANNEL 2

MR. ADAMS AND EVE
TONIGHT AT 9 ON CHANNEL 2

7:30 TONIGHT
PERRY MASON
STARRING RAYMOND BURR
PREMIERE ON CHANNEL 2
CBS TELEVISION

card he once submitted to his superior—the President of the Division. It came back by messenger with a note saying "I don't like it very much. Let's discuss." Bill's answer was simply to scotchtape a drawing pencil to the corner of a large layout pad and send it back with this message scribbled across the top sheet: "Let's not. Why don't you make a better one." There was no reply. The rate card was produced as originally designed.

Bill flatly refused to submit art for approval to anyone. On another occasion, he commissioned the artist René Bouché to do a drawing of a certain television star for a newspaper ad. When the star saw the sketch in the paper he exploded. He demanded that only authorized photographs be used in all future ads. I was one of many who urged Bill not to make an issue of the matter but to go along with the request. Instead, Bill immediately commissioned Bouché to do another drawing of the same performer and again refused to show it to the star. Eventually the new sketch appeared in another ad and became the famous trademark—on the air and off—of America's all-time favorite comedian: Jack Benny.

And so it went for 23 years. A thousand battles. A thousand scars. But never a negotiated peace for the sake of expediency. And simply because he cared so much, fought so hard, and performed so well, he prevailed and was able to give to CBS advertising a dis-

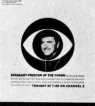

tinction and quality second to none.

I think it is clear by now that Bill was a man of many paradoxes. For example: the less time he spent at the drawing board the greater contribution he made to advertising.

The reason was that he was one of a very small band of pioneers who more than 20 years ago demanded that an art director be more than an ad illustrator . . . that he should participate not only in the design but in the entire process of creating an advertising piece from the moment of conception to the final publication or mailing. He opened new doors to the Art Department and challenged the artist to think, not only about the problems of his craft, but also about the problems of the industry and company for which he worked. It is significant that Bill's title was not Art Director but Creative Director, responsible not alone for design, but for concept and copy as well. And it was his ability in all these areas that made him such a giant in his field.

Still another paradox was his relationship to his staff: he commanded the unswerving loyalty of a staff that was always on the verge of quitting. Each man recognized Bill's ability, his integrity, his willingness to do battle for what they all believed in. Yet much as they admired him, there wasn't a man who didn't say at least twice a year: "I've had it. I'm going to quit."

The loyalty and the resentment both sprang from the same source: simply that Bill demanded the best out of a

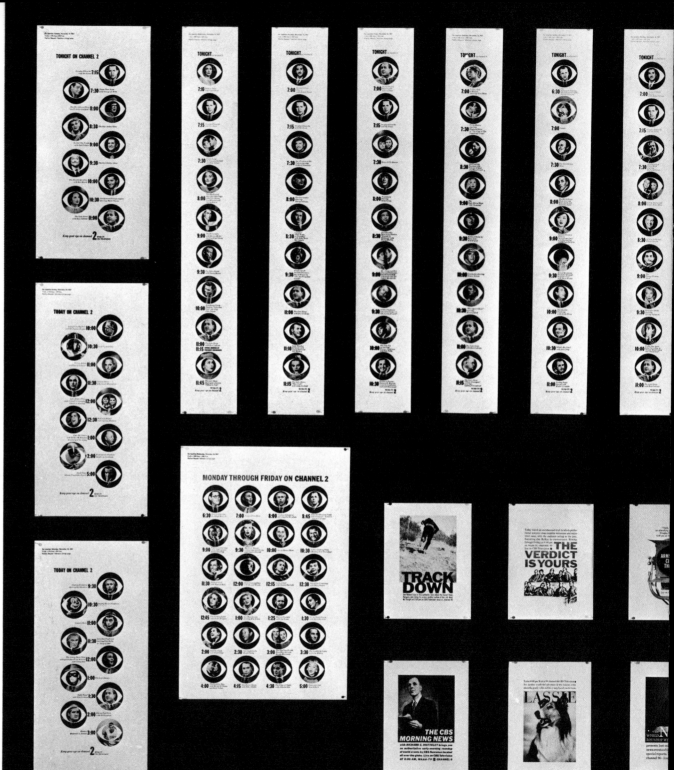

man. Frequently the man did not know how good his best could be until, under Bill's pressure, he extended himself above and beyond what he considered to be the call of duty. Bill achieved this by forcing each man on his staff to undertake what Judge Learned Hand has called "the intolerable task of thinking."

And Bill himself set a dizzying pace. He had the ability to grasp a complicated problem, strip it down to its bare bones, and then come up with a deceptively simple solution. And he backed this ability with long hours of hard work. For example, when Bill turned down the offer of the vice presidency, the company countered with a whopping salary increase. He refused that, too. He said he would rather take Fridays off. It was a wonderful arrangement—for the company. Bill worked with incredible concentration at the office from Monday through late Thursday night, and then took a jam-packed briefcase home and worked all weekend.

This concentration—this infinite capacity for taking pains and attending to detail — was immediately visible whenever you walked into his office. There he was—magnifying glass in hand, bending over a proof like a jeweler over a diamond. Reworking a layout 20 different ways until he decided on the best way. Editing or re-writing version after version of a piece of copy. Tracing by hand each character in a line of copy to assure the proper line break and avoid a widow. Arguing far

WORLD NEWS ROUNDUP

Featuring on-the-spot reports by CBS News correspondents

odyssey

FOR SALE

SATURDAY, JANUARY 12
DETROIT RED WINGS VS
NEW YORK RANGERS AT
2:00 PM ON CHANNEL 2

HOCKEY

NEWS 2

The Jimmy Dean Show

THE CBS MORNING NEWS
WITH RICHARD C. HOTTELET

THE JIMMY DEAN SHOW

PERRY MASON

The Search
STARRING
MONTGOMERY CLIFT
SATURDAY MARCH 9
AT 11:15 PM ON
The Late Show
Channel 2

CAMERA THREE
presents THE ALCHEMY OF LIGHT
a fascinating study of the uses of light in
creation and in art. 11:30 to 12:00 noon
Sunday, March 17, WCBS-TV Channel 2

CHAMPIONSHIP
COLLEGE
BASKETBALL,
CHANNEL 2

CAMILLE

PEOPLE & PLACES

THE GATOR BOWL GAME

THE EDGE OF NIGHT

SUSAN'S SHOW

TOP NEWS
Peter Thomas
Richard C. Hottelet
Walter Cronkite
Robert Trout
Douglas Edwards
Ron Cochran
CHANNEL 2

IF YOU HAD A MILLION

THE ALUMINUM BOWL

HOTEL COSMOPOLITAN

THE VERDICT IS YOURS

NOW SIX DAYS A WEEK

THE JIMMY DEAN SHOW

Good afternoon!

AS THE WORLD TURNS

JANUARY 1, 1958
THE ORANGE BOWL GAME
CBS TELEVISION

THE MASTERS GOLF TOURNAMENT

THE ANTOINETTE PERRY AWARDS

STAY AHEAD OF THE GAME

IF YOU HAD A MILLION

The Jimmy Dean Show

EMP

the garry moore show

9:00
9:30
10:00
10:30
11:30

The Stu Erwin Show
every Monday through Friday

HIGH WALL
THE LATE SHOW
SUNDAY 11:15 PM
CHANNEL 2

MOULIN ROUGE
THE LATE SHOW
WCBS-TV

into the night the relative merits of two alternate headlines. Summarily rejecting an obvious gimmick as an easy but banal solution for a design problem. Searching out hour after hour a graphic concept in which the layout could make a functional contribution to the idea of the advertisement.

Such was his absorption that I recall many late winter afternoons when he was completely oblivious to the fact that he was working in almost total darkness—never thinking to turn on the lights. I can only say that he could accomplish in the dark what few could approximate in the full light of day.

It was, I believe, essentially this extraordinary quality of devotion that Bill gave to his job that earned for him the admiration and respect of his fellow workers. It was also this same intensity of concern that often made him appear a complete stranger to his staff. When examining an idea, or reading a piece of copy, or analyzing a layout—the product was everything, the producer nothing. Indeed, there were times when he scarcely seemed to remember whom he was talking to.

Yet, if Bill happened to learn that a man had a personal problem or was sick or in trouble, he'd stew and fret, offer money, phone and write. It was this curious combination of the impersonal and the highly personal that frequently made him an enigma to his staff.

But there was one thing which all those who worked closely with him agreed about: he had a greater impact

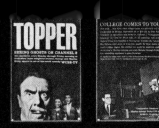

on their careers than almost anyone they ever met. He was a constant source of speculation, a favorite topic of conversation. I recall one occasion when a group of us sat down to lunch and someone said: "Shall we order first, or start talking about Bill right away?"

Another paradox about him was that he was a teacher who never taught. He would give a man a job, and turn him loose without any guidance. When the job came back, he would edit the copy or change the layout—but he would never explain why. It proved to be a most effective technique for it forced each man to learn in the best possible way—by teaching himself.

Last month, at the 39th Annual Meeting of the New York Art Directors Club, Mrs. Golden accepted a special award in Bill's name. But the exhibition itself proved the greatest tribute of all. Thirty-four of the ads and mailing pieces displayed at the exhibition—including six Gold Medals and Distinctive Merit Awards—were designed by men who had once worked for Bill—and who had taught themselves the Golden touch.

Perhaps it can best be summed up in the words of the famous author of *The Education of Henry Adams*. "A teacher" he said, "walks with eternity, for who can say where, or how many generations hence, his influence may be carrying on, unchanged, undiminished, and indestructible."

Bill Golden's influence has only begun.

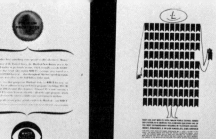

WELCOME ADDITION

1957

PROGRESS REPORT

KNXT

WXIX

EWS PHOTO

WHCT NEWS ◉18

SHOWCASE ◉18

INSIDE ◉18 ◉18

EWS PHOTO

Good Steer

WXIX

What's up in Hartford?

What's up in Hartford? **What's happening in Hartford?** **What's the word in Hartford?** **Heard about Hartford?**

PUBLIC NOTICE

WXIX

GO PLACES WITH PANORAMA PACIFIC!

CBS TELEVISION PACIFIC NETWORK

PRIZE PACKAGE

KNXT

Why all the fireworks

(In June 1959 PRINT Magazine, a bi-monthly publication concerned with graphic design, devoted its issue to the subject of the corporate image in American industry. It included the following article by Mr. Golden.)

My eye

A trademark does not in itself constitute a corporate image. As I understand the phrase (which is rapidly becoming as tedious as "group think" or "creativity") it is the total impression a company makes on the public through its products, its policies, its actions and its advertising effort. I suppose a trademark can serve as a reminder of a corporate image, if you have one.

The "image" of the CBS Television Network would undoubtedly be a strong one even if it undertook no advertising in print, since its "product" is before your eye so often.

If you like the programs it broadcasts, you probably think of its symbol as a good one. If you don't, the symbol would represent something distasteful to you.

Our "service mark" as the lawyers refer to it, was conceived primarily for on-the-air use. It made its first appearance as a still composite photo of the "eye" and a cloud formation photographed from an abandoned Coast Guard

tower. (You would imagine that a cloud picture is the easiest stock photo to find, but it came as a shock to me that there are almost no useful ones.) It was originally conceived as a symbol in motion. It consisted of several concentric "eyes." The camera dollied in to reveal the "pupil" as an iris diaphragm shutter which clicked open to show the network identification and clicked shut.

To guard against possible monotony, three other versions were prepared. One was essentially the still photo with moving clouds, and the other two I've forgotten. Operationally it became necessary to simplify the scheduling to the point where the still has been used most often. Currently the iris diaphragm appears more frequently and it now opens on a photo of coming attractions, clicks again and reveals a program title. The title is not designed by us. The symbol is used in print with the company signatures. It is sometimes used as the principal illustration, in a variety of ways. It appears on studio marquees, trucks, mobile units, cameras, theatre curtains, on the exterior of our building in Television City, Hollywood, in metal, on an interior lobby wall in concrete tile, stenciled on the back of flats and lighting equipment, on matchboxes, ash trays, neckties, cuff links of inlaid marble, press release forms, rate cards, booklets and in the advertising of affiliated stations. Hardly a month goes by without someone suggesting a new use for it. But we try to avoid forcing it where it doesn't belong, and even in printed advertising it is omitted whenever it conflicts with the rest of the design.

We also try to keep affiliated stations from misusing it, but I'm afraid this is something of a losing battle. It's amazing to me how easily it can be made to look repulsive.

It is used so often that it sometimes seems like a Franken-

stein to me, but I am grateful it is such a versatile thing t~~h~~
there seems to be no end to the number of ways it can be u~~s~~
without losing its identity.

The function of the symbol was not only to differentiate
from the other television networks, but from our own rad~~io~~
network as well.

It was first designed when CBS established the Radio a~~nd~~
Television Networks as two separate divisions. The two ne~~t~~
works were urged to do everything possible to create the~~ir~~
own identities. This was a time, too, when television, thou~~gh~~
still in the red, was obviously becoming important. The aud~~i~~
ence was growing like wildfire, and with more and more eye~~s~~
focused on the television screen, everyone was becoming mor~~e~~
concerned with the quality of the images that were broadcast~~.~~

To tell the truth, I had submitted three identifications to ~~a~~
dozen or so people who attended the original viewing. I can't
report that any of them—including the "eye"—were received
with uncontrollable enthusiasm by the group.

But one man's reaction was immediate and decisive. And
that was Frank Stanton, the president of CBS. In fact, a year
later, when I timidly suggested we abandon it and do something else (for in this world of "showbusiness," you are under
constant temptation to change for the sake of change alone)
he reminded me of an old advertising axiom. Just when you're
beginning to get bored with what you have done is probably
the time it is beginning to be noticed by your audience.

So I suspect that the keen eye of Stanton and his sensible
decision to stay with it, are more responsible for the success
of the "eye" than I am.